WE NEED TO TALK ABOUT INFLATION

WE NEED TO TALK ABOUT INFLATION

14 URGENT LESSONS FROM
THE LAST 2,000 YEARS

STEPHEN D. KING

YALE UNIVERSITY PRESS
NEW HAVEN AND LONDON

For information about this and other Yale University Press publications, please contact:
U.S. Office: sales.press@yale.edu   yalebooks.com
Europe Office: sales@yaleup.co.uk   yalebooks.co.uk

Set in Adobe Caslon Pro by IDSUK (DataConnection) Ltd
Printed in Great Britain by TJ Books, Padstow, Cornwall

Library of Congress Control Number: 2023931517

ISBN 978-0-300-27047-1

A catalogue record for this book is available from the British Library.

10 9 8 7 6 5 4 3 2 1

To the memory – and belated discovery – of the mysterious
Mary Slattery

Contents

Figures and Tables

Figures

Tables

Acknowledgements

A few of the ideas behind *We Need to Talk About Inflation* emerged in the months before I embarked on writing the book itself. I had composed a number of articles for *HSBC Research* and columns for the *Evening Standard* regarding aspects of what I perceived to be a rising inflationary threat. I was aware, however, that any useful book about inflation would inevitably have to offer an extended historical narrative, at the very least to highlight issues unfamiliar to many people today. I was also keen to gain insights from those whose job it had been to defeat inflation or, at the very least, keep it at bay.

I am, thus, enormously grateful to those from the policy-making 'coalface' who read and commented on the entire manuscript. Mervyn King, Terry Burns and Alan Budd (to be more formal, Lord King of Lothbury KG GBE, Lord Burns of Pitshanger GCB and Sir Alan Budd GBE), all at the centre of UK economic policymaking at one point or another over the years, provided incredibly useful guidance and advice. It was with huge sadness that I learnt of Alan's passing in January 2023: he had been a tremendous source of support throughout and I shall very much miss his wit, enthusiasm and generosity.

Colleagues at HSBC were also kind enough to read every page. Janet Henry, HSBC's global chief economist, went one stage further: in 2021, she was my co-author on an HSBC note, 'The creation of inflation: "looking through" versus "it's coming back"'. Other HSBC colleagues offering sage advice included Simon Wells (ex-Bank of England) and Murat Ulgen, an expert on inflationary episodes in emerging markets and the source of my Turkish washing machine story. Ryan Wang and James Pomeroy were useful foils for some of my more controversial ideas. Chris Brown-Humes, formerly of HSBC and now worrying about the impact of inflation on his pension, was kind enough to cast his beady editor's eye across the book as a whole.

I have had many conversations with others who, whether or not they knew where I was heading, have undoubtedly helped strengthen the book's arguments. Peter Oppenheimer, chief global equity strategist at Goldman Sachs, helped me clarify plausible investment options during periods of high inflation. Stephen Grosz, the renowned psychoanalyst and author of *The Examined Life*, offered tremendous insights regarding group-think, committee construction and the varying psychological qualities of committee chairs. Paul Tucker, formerly deputy governor of the Bank of England and now an acclaimed author and academic, provided excellent advice regarding both quantitative easing (and its relationship with fiscal policy) and decision making at the Bank of England. Richard Cookson, a columnist at Bloomberg and a friend since student days, kept me on my inflationary toes throughout.

I have also benefited from comments from various 'anonymous referees', either during the planning stage or at the very end of the process: whoever the latter was – and I have my suspicions – knows their economic history very well indeed. Others who have chipped in with ideas include Bernard Shapero (from Shapero Rare Books), who reminded me about Weimar's King of Inflation, and Charlie Bean, professor of economics at the LSE and another former deputy governor of the Bank of England, who talked about not just fiscal dominance but also the potential for 'financial dominance'.

I'm indebted to Claudio Borio and Hyun Song Shin for inviting me to speak about inflation at the (sadly virtual) Bank for International Settlements' private sector chief economists' round-table in spring 2022. The meeting helped crystallise my thinking regarding Taylor rules and other alternative ways of setting policy rates. As ever, I must thank the Centre for European Reform for inviting me to take part in their annual conferences at Ditchley Park in Oxfordshire: the 2022 version cheerfully focused on war, pandemics and inflation. My role on the Council of Management of the National Institute of Economic and Social Research has given me access to the considerable talents of Jagjit Chadha and his team. As a director of Henderson Eurotrust, I have witnessed at first hand how inflationary uncertainty complicates the lives of investors. And, although I'm not sure I won over the entire audience – or, for that matter, my fellow panellists – I enjoyed debating all things inflationary at the Society of Professional Economists' annual conference in November 2022.

I work only part-time at HSBC nowadays, but, despite my part-time status, I have continued to benefit from the bank's support. Kathryn Gurney was enthusiastic from the very beginning. Mark Tucker, Noel Quinn, Steve John, Tim Rowbottom, Pam Kaur, Georges Elhedery, Stephen Moss, Patrick George, Sherard Cowper-Coles, Helen Belopolsky and David May have all been helpful in one way or another. I offer particular thanks to Debbie Falcus, my long-suffering executive assistant, who continues to manage my working life in ways that I simply couldn't manage on my own.

Everyone connected to Yale University Press has, as before, been incredibly encouraging. Julian Loose, my editor, has been with me all the way, supportive of what has been an unusually tight timetable by book standards. Frazer Martin, Rachael Lonsdale and Heather Nathan have all made my life a lot easier. I'm also very grateful to Clive Liddiard for his copy-editing skills and Ruth Killick for her marketing talents.

Last, but by no means least, I have to thank my wonderful wife, Yvonne, and our three children, Helena, Olivia and Sophie. My daughters may now all be adults, but they're not old enough to have experienced the traumas associated with a sustained period of inflation. For their sakes, I hope this book will add something to the debate, in the process reducing the risks of a repetition of past policy errors.

London, January 2023

Preface: The Journey from Deflation to Inflation

The unimaginable re-emergence of inflation – the 'Japanese problem' era – a deflationary fetish – my four fears

From deflation to inflation

In 2021, inflation emerged from a multi-decade hibernation. At first, policymakers convinced themselves that rising prices were restricted to only a few limited areas, most obviously secondhand cars and semiconductors, a consequence of Covid-19-related global supply shortages. Other prices were, apparently, still 'well behaved'. As such, central bankers were unwilling to raise interest rates even as inflation accelerated. In their view, inflation would disappear in short order.

Yet, rather than disappearing, inflation accelerated further. While President Putin's decision to invade Ukraine – with all its consequences for energy prices – provided a convenient rationale for inflation rates not seen since the 1970s (or, in some cases, even earlier), this was not the whole story. Price pressures were emerging across a multitude of different areas. Labour markets were, in many cases, unusually 'tight', with vacancies surging and wages accelerating. On some measures, 'real' interest rates (actual interest rates minus the rate of inflation) were tumbling, suggesting that 'independent' central banks were repeating the mistakes of their political forefathers fifty years earlier. After a while, those who ignored these increasingly febrile inflationary conditions were in danger of receiving from the markets the financial equivalent of a bloody nose.[1]

The re-emergence of inflation represents something of a watershed moment in the development of the global economy. For much of the last three decades, both policy-makers and investors focused much more on the dangers of deflation, a world in which prices and wages threatened to fall rather than rise, and in which interest rates could drop to zero or marginally below. There was a growing sense that developed nations were experiencing an economic 'Japanification'. As such, inflation's return was not just unlikely, but unimaginable.

Admittedly, Japan's fall from economic grace in the 1990s was, at first, regarded as a 'special case', a story that had few parallels elsewhere. Yet following the collapse of the US tech bubble in 2000 and, eight years later, the onset of the Global Financial Crisis, what was initially regarded as a 'Japanese problem' took on a whole new international dimension. In both Europe and North America, populations were ageing; debts were rising; asset prices were – initially – tumbling; banks were failing; growth was stagnating; and, in an increasing number of cases, prices were falling.

The resurrection of inflation

In these circumstances, old battles against inflation which had formed the dominant economic narrative of the 1970s and 1980s became no more than distant memories. I was certainly one of those who initially thought the only monetary threat now came from deflation or, at the very least, excessively low inflation. Yet, as time went by, I began to feel increasingly uncomfortable about this 'Japanese-style deflation' narrative. And, as I thought more about the issue, I wondered whether, perhaps, deflation was no longer the only game in town.

My thinking began to coalesce around four fears. First, I wondered whether the low inflation we had witnessed was partly a consequence of benevolent forces stemming from globalisation. Put simply, with capital travelling around the world in search of cheap labour, those of us fortunate enough to live in the developed world could potentially benefit from ever cheaper imports. In these circumstances, prices might fall relative to wages and profits, leading to 'real income' gains. This was a 'good' deflation, similar to that witnessed in the late nineteenth century. If, however, globalisation threatened to go into reverse – as I warned in my last book, *Grave New World* – the risk was that these 'deflationary' gains might turn into 'inflationary' losses.[2]

Second, with the onset of the Covid-19 pandemic, there was a great deal of discussion among economists and policymakers about 'scarring'. The idea was that, even as lockdowns came to an end, economies would be unable to return to 'normal' any time soon: not all economies would reopen at the same time, thereby hampering global supply chains, while the surge in debt levels during the pandemic might impose a deadweight loss on future growth prospects. To me, however, scarring raised important risks that others were ignoring. If 'supply' was unable to keep up with the newly unlocked 'demand', inflation might be the natural consequence. Meanwhile, for governments keen to 'build back better', getting rid of debts via inflation might prove to be a politically expedient, if economically undesirable, option.[3]

Third, while the initial collapse in economic activity associated with lockdowns was as big as had been seen during the Great Depression in the early 1930s, the similarities ended there. There were no bank failures, no crunching deflation, no mass bankruptcies and no lasting increase in unemployment. Fiscal policy – in the form of loan guarantees, cash grants and furlough schemes – prevented a collapse of the economic infrastructure. Monetary policy, however, was loosened, as if we were on the verge of another Depression-era financial calamity. When it turned out that we weren't, there was a marked reluctance to tighten (until, from the perspective of price stability, it was too late).

Fourth, it struck me that central banks had complacently taken the view that, whatever happened in the near term, their policies would remain credible in the eyes of the public and that, as such, there was little chance of inflation running amok. This, I thought, represented a serious misreading of history, and is one reason why this book delves into the past to cast light on the inflationary problems that have emerged during the pandemic and its aftermath. Blaming President Putin is, more than anything, an *ex post* act of convenience (following a pattern established by policymakers, most visibly in the early 1970s). Yes, inflation would have been lower had Russia not invaded Ukraine. It would not, however, have returned to 'target'.

I summarised some of these views in an article I penned for the London *Evening Standard* in May 2021.[4] I wasn't the only person expressing my concerns regarding inflation: Larry

Summers, former US treasury secretary, and Jason Furman, former chair of the president's Council of Economic Advisers, had issued warnings about rising inflationary pressures in the US;[5] and Martin Wolf was writing articles in the *Financial Times* cautioning about a return of inflation at the global level.[6] Roger Bootle, who had once signalled the 'Death of Inflation', began to write about its resurrection. Andy Haldane, the Bank of England's chief economist, warned in February 2021 that inflationary risks were skewed to the upside. Earlier still, Richard Cookson, on behalf of Bloomberg, had composed robust attacks on those content to ignore signs of an emerging inflationary problem.[7]

In the *Evening Standard* article, I wrote that 'there are plenty of people who believe that the recent inflationary up-tick will peter out in a few months. Chief among them are the world's central bankers.' I added that 'our policymakers are keeping the monetary and fiscal sluices wide open ... [yet] as with the early-Seventies, it may be that the economic rules of the game have changed ... These are the kinds of conditions in which policymakers make mistakes, wedded to a version of the world that may no longer exist.'

Those mistakes are now a lot more obvious, even if many central bankers – and, for that matter, many economists more generally – believe current excessive inflation rates will simply fade away, never to reappear. Why, however, were the siren voices ignored? What went wrong? Was it a failure of central banks alone, or were central bankers merely pawns on a chessboard upon which politicians were demanding a greater tolerance of inflation? If so, what might that tolerance mean for living standards, for income and wealth inequality, for central banks themselves and for political stability in coming years?

After a scene-setting introduction, my book covers (i) the history of inflation and its relationship with money; (ii) the printing press and its temptations; (iii) inflation's deeply undemocratic effects; and (iv) the difficulties associated with inflation's removal. I then take a close look at recent failures and offer four 'tests' which central bankers and other policy-makers should ideally adopt. I conclude with what I consider to be fourteen urgent lessons (taken from two thousand years of history) and offer thoughts on how, in the future, we might manage inflationary risks a little better.

Others have warned about a return of inflation based on rather different reasons, most obviously the impact of population ageing on the price of labour. I have mostly steered clear from such 'shock' arguments, partly because they have yet to apply to Japan, a country that found itself unable to create meaningful inflation despite such demographic pressures.[8] Instead, I have focused much more on the role of central banks, money, governments, and political preferences.

While inflation has been dormant on many occasions, it has never truly died. As I write, inflation is going through yet another resurrection. Understanding why this is happening and what needs to be done about it are two of the biggest economic – and, indeed, political – questions of our time.

1

The Resurrection of Inflation

Reflections on a 1970s childhood – distortions in downtown Istanbul – undermining the price mechanism – excusing the post-pandemic inflationary surge – fearing deflation more than inflation

From historical relic to harsh reality

From the late 1980s onwards, inflation was increasingly regarded as a historical relic. After short-lived inflationary skirmishes in the late 1940s and early 1950s, prices began to rise more rapidly in the late 1960s and, even more so, in the 1970s. Thereafter, however, most of us got used to a world of 'price stability'.[1] Admittedly, there were some dishonourable exceptions: inflationary excesses in Argentina and Turkey; and outright hyperinflation in post-war Hungary, the former Soviet states and, more recently, Venezuela and Zimbabwe. As time went by, however, it seemed as though policymakers had

1

finally worked out how best to prevent prices and wages from surging in seemingly relentless fashion. Indeed, at times it appeared that policymakers had been *too* successful: after the 2008 Global Financial Crisis, deflation – a world of *falling* prices and wages – was regarded as the bigger threat, with widely shared fears that the western developed world was in danger of emulating deflationary Japan's decades-long battle against perceived economic stagnation.[2]

Yet, as I began writing this book, inflation was making an unwelcome return. Worse, as the months went past and the chapters piled up, inflation headed still higher. Policymakers couldn't agree on why inflation was back. Some blamed the Covid-19 pandemic. Others blamed President Putin. Few, however, were prepared to admit that inflation's return was, perhaps, a reflection of a more deep-rooted problem. Central bankers' forecasts of inflation suggested that any near-term increase would be transitory: within two or three years, inflation would return to 'target' – in most cases a number close to 2 per cent. Most other forecasters agreed. A return to the inflationary past was not just unlikely but, it seemed, unimaginable.

That conclusion, however, may represent a serious misreading of history. Inflation may sometimes be dormant, but it has never been banished. It always threatens to return, egged on not so much by the technical monetary skills of those who staff our central banks, but instead by inflation's multifaceted relationship with changing economic and political realities. Inflation can offer what, politically, appears to be the 'easy way out'. In the short term, it is sometimes easier to tolerate inflation than accept the potentially painful consequences of its removal. Longer term, however, such tolerance almost always leads to regret. As I shall argue, inflation is a stealthy but decidedly unpleasant adversary, one that can do untold damage to an economy and to the fabric of our political and institutional life.

Book prices, stickers and pocket money

Before I do so, however, I want to take you back to my childhood. Growing up in the 1970s, I experienced a rather specific – and unpleasant – version of inflation involving the purchase of books and the receipt of pocket money. Every so often, the price of books would rise (yet never fall). I'd sometimes find that the original price printed on the back of a coveted paperback had been covered with a sticker which, in turn, would reveal a new – inevitably higher – price. The temptation to remove the sticker was, of course, very strong; but the adhesive used to attach the sticker was, typically, even stronger. Sometimes, I'd be lucky enough to find a copy without a sticker. For the most part, however, I'd have to regretfully accept that the price was now higher than I had bargained for a few weeks earlier.

This was a sign of inflation. The book might have been printed a year or two earlier, but even though the story, the words, the pages and the cover hadn't changed (apart from the newly affixed sticker), the price was rising nonetheless. To me, living on what I feared was a fixed amount of pocket money, this was not good news. My 'cost of living' was heading upwards, yet my 'wage' was fixed. From the bookseller's or publisher's perspective, however, it appeared to be very good news indeed: stock that had cost a certain amount to produce in, say, 1972 could be sold at a much higher price in 1974 (admittedly, a publisher's costs or a bookseller's rent might have risen in the intervening period, implying that any paper 'gains' could have been siphoned off via a higher wage bill or by an avaricious landlord: that, however, was not my problem).

In truth, it wasn't so much that books were becoming more expensive relative to, for example, sofas, cameras or a joint of beef: rather, money was losing its value relative to books and virtually anything else that could be bought in the shops. If there had been a healthy secondhand market for Enid Blyton's efforts, I might have taken advantage. I could have speculatively hung on to my collection of *Famous Five* adventures and, having outgrown them, sold them at a higher price a few years later. Yet eBay and the like didn't exist back then, and I couldn't afford to use the expensive (at least, for me) 'classified ads' in a vague attempt to identify a would-be buyer.

Turkish washing machines

Others, however, have dealt with inflation in precisely this way, holding on to goods, as opposed to money, when prices have been rising quickly. During a period of ludicrously high Turkish inflation in the 1990s[3] – one of many such episodes over the years – some Istanbul wholesalers hoarded washing machines, preferring to sell them for a higher price at a later date. Their 'savings' were better protected in the form of kitchen appliances than cash. Meanwhile, those flush with Turkish lira chose to buy small fleets of imported luxury cars to protect their savings. Exchange controls made it difficult for them to swap their lira into inflation-proofed US dollars, Deutsche Marks or sterling. These apparent petrolheads were better off owning a slowly depreciating foreign asset than sitting on a pile of rapidly depreciating domestic cash.

For the overall good of Turkish society, washing machines would have been better deployed in people's homes than in warehouses collecting dust. Fewer imports of BMW coupés and Mercedes-Benz limousines might have helped the Turkish balance of payments. For those eager to protect their 'wealth', however, stockpiles of washing machines and luxury cars were attractive options. Inflation creates very strange incentives, distorting economic decisions in ways that make the otherwise irrational entirely sensible. Take my childhood book-buying experience. To keep up with inflation, someone had to be employed to affix the new price stickers. In the absence of inflation, it's a role that would never have been necessary. In that sense, inflation creates otherwise futile work and leads people to make very odd choices.

Relative price changes

Admittedly, prices change all the time, whether or not inflation is present. Fresh vegetables sold in a street market are typically cheaper towards the end of the day, when the stock needs to be cleared. Algorithms help calculate the 'market-clearing' price for an airline seat at any one moment in time, implying that the price offered tomorrow may differ from the price on offer today. In supermarkets, 'three for the price of two' deals are mechanisms designed to shift unwanted stock. Sometimes, companies will 'raise prices' simply by shrinking the size of a particular product: a Mars bar weighs less today than it did in the 1990s.[4] And, over time, technology has made it easier to change prices on a whim, without the inefficiencies of yesteryear.

Many of the above examples, however, refer to 'relative' price movements: the price of one item rises (or falls) compared with others. In themselves, such price changes are a sign neither of inflation (a world in which prices tend continuously to rise) nor of deflation (a world in which prices tend continuously to fall). They are, instead, examples of Adam Smith's 'invisible hand' at work. As the great Scottish economist and philosopher observed

while caricaturing the motives and the actions of a selfish businessman in his monumental *Wealth of Nations*:

> He generally ... neither intends to promote the public
> interest, nor knows how much he is promoting it ... by
> directing that industry in such a manner as its produce may
> be of the greatest value, he intends only his own gain, and
> he is in this, as in many other cases, led by an invisible hand
> to promote an end which was no part of his intention. Nor
> is it always the worse for the society that it was not part of
> it. By pursuing his own interest he frequently promotes
> that of the society more effectually than when he really
> intends to promote it.[5]

The price mechanism is, in effect, the invisible hand. We all
respond to it, to a greater or lesser extent. If the price of a
particular product rises, as consumers we may buy less, but as
suppliers, we may eventually produce more. Prices provide information about supply and demand across millions of markets
simultaneously. We react to these signals without even thinking
about the consequences. Yet, in responding, we shift not only
our own behaviour, but that of others. Clever mathematical
models show that, under certain key – even if implausible –
assumptions, the price mechanism will deliver the most efficient
economic outcome, in the sense that no one can be made better
off without someone else being made worse off.[6] Importantly,
these models also suggest that other economic arrangements –
such as central planning or, for that matter, the 'non-market'
activities that routinely take place within companies and across
the public sector – will struggle to offer the same level of efficiency. Without price 'information', it's difficult to gauge either
consumer preferences or emerging shortages.

Covid-19 and lost price information

Evidence for the importance of price information emerged – unexpectedly, perhaps – during the Covid-19 pandemic. Multiple lockdowns triggered the closure of multiple markets. By implication, many prices simply weren't available. Some markets disappeared more or less entirely. Restaurants closed for months on end. So did hotels and theatres. Global supply chains fragmented. Foreign workers went home. Other workers retired or moved to the countryside. Recruitment stopped. When lockdowns ended and markets reopened, a peculiar state of 'economic ignorance' was revealed. Underlying supply and demand conditions had undoubtedly changed. Yet many prices had been preserved in aspic from months earlier. Waiters were now in short supply, but waiters' wages were no higher than they had been pre-pandemic. Restaurants offered their customers menus with prices that in no way reflected the new waiter shortage. Flush with cash saved during multiple lockdowns, consumers tried to buy new cars, but a global components shortage led only to lengthening waiting lists and an unprecedented increase in both the demand for and the price of second-hand cars. Because London cabbies who had either retired or changed career had not been replaced with new recruits, would-be passengers were often left stranded as they tried to make their way home on a Saturday night.

The effects of inflation are not quite the same as the effects of lockdown, but nevertheless, the two are intertwined. Most obviously, inflation itself can best be measured if as many markets as possible are 'live', such that prices are constantly being recorded. In the UK, the Office for National Statistics – the body tasked with totting up the monthly inflation data – found itself at a significant disadvantage during the Covid pandemic: some prices were distorted, while more prices than normal had to be imputed. In that sense, inflation data over that period were more of a 'fiction' than usual (and, in 'normal' times, consumer prices are more fictional than might be imagined: in the UK, the price of tools in a standard toolkit is proxied by the price of a screwdriver, even though screwdrivers vary hugely in shape and size).[7]

Even when inflation is 'correctly' measured, it nevertheless offers distortions, which, in turn, prevent us from identifying the true state of economic affairs. It's as if we end up observing the world through a randomly distorting lens, which serves only to undermine our perception of economic reality. In real time, distinguishing between relative price changes (those that represent shortages or abundance) and general price changes (which simply reflect a loss in the value of money relative to everything else) becomes near enough impossible. I experienced this problem as a child. If book prices rose three or four times a year, but my pocket money was lifted just once a year, there would be periods when my spending power would 'fall behind', before (hopefully) catching up and (with luck) overtaking the increase in book prices. In real time, however, I could never be sure whether book prices were rising or falling relative to the price of everything else. In particular, I had no way of knowing whether my pocket money would ultimately increase in line with the rising price of books.

Now imagine repeating this process across society as a whole. Winners and losers emerge, some on a temporary basis, some permanently. Those who lose observe with increasing anger the arbitrary gains made by the lucky winners. Trust across society begins to erode. In effect, inflation works as a mechanism arbitrarily and unfairly to take from some, even while giving to others. Those with only limited cash savings –

notably the poor and pensioners – tend to be hit particularly hard, lacking as they do the financial depth and knowledge to 'protect' their savings. Those who have borrowed heavily – governments, house purchasers, some businesses – may eventually emerge as winners: even if the cost of borrowing rises, their debts will likely diminish over time relative to their now inflating incomes. Unionised labour – able to strike at the drop of a hat – can often succeed in negotiating an 'inflation-busting' wage increase. Those working on their own or in a small business are more likely to find their wages simply can't keep up. Dominant companies can easily pass cost increases (and more) onto their customers, but suppliers to those companies or those who find themselves in some other highly competitive environment will fare less well.

All societies produce winners and losers, at least in relative terms. To a degree, this process is both understandable and tolerable. Most of us don't tend to lose a lot of sleep over the accumulated riches of Elon Musk or Jeff Bezos (although we might object to the accumulated wealth of kleptocratic dictators). We also, however reluctantly, recognise that some industries – and the people they employ – may fall on hard times. We hope to tackle the consequences of these inequalities of wealth, income and opportunity through state intervention, ranging from public ownership in a command economy through to contingent tax and benefit arrangements in an otherwise free-market economy.

Lenin's 'debauchery'

Inflation, however, is a much more random and arbitrary way of creating winners and losers. It is, in effect, an undemocratic process, one reason why John Maynard Keynes claimed during Treaty of Versailles negotiations that:

> Lenin is said to have declared that the best way to destroy the Capitalist System was to debauch the currency. By a continuing process of inflation, Governments can confiscate, secretly and unobserved, an important part of the wealth of their citizens.[8]

Whether or not Lenin actually claimed as such is neither here nor there (his preferred course of revolutionary action appears to have been a combination of violence *and* the printing press: although data are hard to come by, inflation in the fledgling Soviet Union appears to have been stratospheric). And we will never know whether Lenin fully recognised that, in a democracy, a government that chooses the path of inflation can be voted out of office. Nevertheless, what is most probably an apocryphal story still contains an element of truth. Inflation can, indeed, benefit the government finances, effectively by acting as a stealthy tax on wealth. Those whose savings are in cash or low-yielding government bonds are particularly vulnerable. Over time, their claims on real resources will dwindle. Meanwhile, the government's finances will improve: the value of existing government debt will fall relative to a national income that is 'inflating' higher, while the interest paid on that debt will become less and less burdensome, so long as the inflation rate is above the interest rate (in which case, the so-called 'real' interest rate is negative).

There are plentiful examples of such inflationary kleptocracy. Many are associated with situations in which political ambition or constraint clashes with economic or diplomatic reality. Prime examples include the German and Austrian hyperinflations after the First World War and, over many decades, ongoing battles between successive Buenos Aires governments and Argentina's domestic and foreign creditors. Many such episodes reveal that inflation is much more than just a technical process in which overly loose monetary policy leads to rising wages and prices. From a near-term political perspective, inflation can be seen as a means of escape, a way of imposing taxes 'secretly' on those with savings. As Edmund de Waal memorably describes in *The Hare with Amber Eyes*,[9] the Viennese branch of the Ephrussi family – a wealthy Jewish dynasty that originally made its fortune from commodity trading in the Black Sea, before migrating to western Europe – patriotically thanked its adopted homeland by investing the bulk of its wealth in Austro-Hungarian war bonds. The Viennese Ephrussis were left more or less penniless in the aftermath of the First World War, as inflation destroyed the value of their nominal holdings. Worse, their financial patriotism turned out to be of zero benefit to them in the 1920s, a decade in which antisemitism tragically became a politically viable option across much of Europe.

Losing faith

Such kleptocratic inflationary behaviour has consequences. In their desire to accept just a little bit of inflation to help the fiscal arithmetic, governments and central banks are likely to trigger compensating behaviour from their citizens. Put simply, the danger is that people lose faith in their monetary and fiscal masters. In doing so, they increasingly try to rid themselves of money. Why, after all, keep something which the government is effectively guaranteeing will lose value over time? In a world of floating currencies, and in the absence of exchange and capital controls, the most immediate way in which this occurs is via the foreign exchange markets: if one currency is not trusted as much as others, it is likely to fall in value, as those with spare cash swap their assets into 'safer' currencies. That decline increases import prices in the 'devaluing' nation (more domestic currency now has to be spent to buy a given amount of foreign currency), which may, in turn, lead to more generalised domestic inflation. Retailers will attempt to pass on higher import prices in the form of higher selling prices. Workers will demand compensation for such price increases via higher wages.

If, under these circumstances, the government or central bank stands idly by, seemingly indifferent to a currency's decline on the foreign exchanges, a point may be reached where currency rejection increasingly becomes a domestic, as well as an international, problem. That rejection is reflected in a desire to get rid of domestic cash balances as quickly as possible, typically either by switching into a 'hard' foreign currency or, as in Turkey's 1990s experience, by acquiring 'physical' inflation-proof assets. This, however, becomes a self-fulfilling process. Imagine, for example, that many people in the United States fear a sustained rise in inflation, reflecting a common perception of widespread official complacency regarding the achievement of price stability. If enough of those people then decide to swap their cash savings into durable goods, prices of durables will rise and shelves will empty. At some point, the authorities may decide to 'print' more money, hoping that sufficient funds will be created to allow demand to rise to meet the new, higher prices. Unfortunately, doing so will only serve to reinforce people's perceptions that the authorities are not serious about stabilising the currency's domestic value. People might then endeavour to rid themselves of remaining currency even faster than before. Eventually, what started off as a fear of currency debauchery would become a hyperinflationary reality. Periods of hyperinflation are not simply stories about the printing of money. As we shall see, they also reflect a collapse in trust regarding money, both as a store of value and as a medium of exchange.

Not everyone wants hyperinflation

It would be foolish to claim that every instance of inflation turns into hyperinflation, in which money loses value at a catastrophic pace. Hyperinflations are enormously damaging, threatening revolution and untold political violence. Most governments and central banks do enough to prevent such terrible outcomes. Proving that they are not in the business of destroying the currency is not, however, the same thing as stabilising the currency's value. There are many outcomes between these two extremes. And those outcomes can vary over time. During the 1970s, inflation in some countries was seen as an unfortunate affliction that had to be tolerated because, at the time, the bigger priority was the desire to reduce unemployment. For that generation of policymakers, it was an understandable ambition: they, after all, had grown up in the 1930s Depression and were haunted by the memory of truly mass unemployment. Yet, as the 1970s progressed, it became increasingly clear that, without tackling inflation, there was no easy way of reducing unemployment. That required an intellectual revolution within policy circles and, eventually, a radical change in political priorities – things that were unlikely to take place overnight. And nor did they.

Identifying periods of inflation is, in hindsight, a relatively straightforward exercise. In many cases – particularly since the beginning of the twentieth century – data are reliable enough to demonstrate when inflation has been present. Sometimes, however, nations 'hide' their inflation, hoping that an official denial will be good enough to keep a lid on inflationary fears. Ironically, those who go down this path are typically those with the worst possible inflation records. During the presidency of Cristina Fernández de Kirchner (2007–2015), Argentine statisticians were, in effect, instructed to 'massage' Argentina's inflation data to make inflation appear to be better behaved than it actually was. Earning the opprobrium of, among others, the International Monetary Fund (IMF), the 'cover-up' only served to undermine trust in the monetary and fiscal authorities still further.[10] For the record, Argentine average annual inflation was 9.2 per cent between 2007 and 2013 and, according to the IMF, 132 per cent between 2013 and 2020.

Taking credit for price stability: our now-tarnished monetary masters

Yet even if we can confidently separate periods of inflation (and, for that matter, deflation) from periods of price stability, it's not quite so straightforward to explain why the transition from stability to instability takes place. In recent decades, many have regarded inflation as a series of stories from a bygone age. Yes, some of the world's poorer nations remain vulnerable to inflationary problems; but for North America, much of Europe and, most obviously, Japan, inflation had supposedly receded into the policy background. The political temptation to create inflation had been removed through the establishment of independent central banks, which have mostly been tasked with delivering price stability. Central bankers, meanwhile, have been happy to take much of the credit for delivering this. In 2004, two years before becoming chair of the Federal Reserve, Ben Bernanke – a mere member of the Federal Reserve Board at the time – argued that:

> monetary policy has likely made an important contribution not only to the reduced volatility of inflation (which is not particularly controversial) but to the reduced volatility of output as well . . . [I am] optimistic for the future, because

14

I am confident that monetary policymakers will not forget the lessons of the 1970s.[11]

That optimism has gone awry on at least two counts. First, the 2008 Global Financial Crisis revealed that economic collapse was possible even when inflation had apparently been tamed. Any economic historian worth their salt already knew this – for example, there wasn't much in the way of inflation ahead of the 1929 Wall Street Crash and the Great Depression that followed two years later – so it's surprising that Bernanke, an expert on US economic events in the 1930s, chose not to highlight the connection. Second, the huge upside inflationary surprises since the onset of the Covid-19 pandemic seriously undermine the idea that inflation is merely a challenge to be handled smoothly by central banking technicians. If it was, how could it have risen so quickly? Why was Jerome Powell, the chair of the Federal Reserve, forced to stop describing inflation as 'transitory', an admission that inflation was proving to be a rather thornier problem than had hitherto been recognised? Why was it that, in the UK, an apparently temporary phenomenon rapidly morphed into a 'cost-of-living crisis'? Why did deflationary Europe turn on a sixpence – or should that be a euro? – to become inflationary Europe?

The post-pandemic inflationary surge

It's worth placing the inflationary shocks emerging from the pandemic in a historical context. In 2021, US inflation averaged 7.0 per cent, the highest outcome since 1981. UK inflation averaged a much more soporific 2.6 per cent that year – only marginally above the 2 per cent official target – before heading into double digits in late 2022, the highest rate since the early

1980s. Eurozone inflation also reached double digits in late 2022, the highest rate since data were first collected in the late 1990s. For Germany alone, inflation was probably at its highest since the formation of the Federal Republic in 1949.[12]

Inflation at these rates was near enough unthinkable within the economic forecasting community. Whatever the cause of such increases, there was a collective failure of imagination in perceiving the risk in the first place. In all three geographies, inflation ended up higher than even the very highest forecasts made a few months earlier. Month after month, in a seemingly relentless fashion, inflation came in ahead of expectations.

Of course, it's easy to 'excuse' such outcomes on the basis of near-term pandemic-related supply constraints and the impact on energy and food prices of Russia's 2022 invasion of Ukraine. Central banks have been quick with such excuses, arguing that much of the increase in inflation has very little to do with monetary policy and a great deal to do with what might loosely be described as 'bad luck'. So confident were central bankers that inflation would ultimately come back to heel that, in the initial stages of the inflationary surge, they left interest rates well alone: the first, modest, increases occurred only at the very end of 2021 and the beginning of 2022.

Even then, the gap between the inflation rate and policy rates at times continued to widen. Interest rates may have been rising, but they were not rising anywhere near as quickly as inflation. The reluctance to tighten monetary conditions undoubtedly reflected a perception that the rise in inflation was, indeed, temporary. Supporting evidence came from measures of infla-tionary expectations, which for a while appeared to be relatively stable, suggesting that both the public and participants in financial markets were as relaxed about inflation as the central bankers were.

Public confidence can fade faster than official confidence

These views, however, deserve to be treated with a healthy degree of scepticism. As history demonstrates all too often, public confidence in a currency – and confidence in those tasked with managing it – can shift remarkably quickly. Policymakers with the best of intentions can still be fallible – particularly those who fall for groupthink, who complacently ignore lessons from history or, indeed, misinterpret those lessons. And the fact that central bankers are 'independent' does not guarantee immunity from political influence. Politicians can – and have – adjusted central bank mandates. Politicians typically appoint a central bank's key decision makers. And the central bankers themselves know that a failure to heed political 'realities' might ultimately lead to a loss of independence or, at the very least, a failure to be reappointed for a second term in office.

Worse, central bankers are sometimes faced with an uncomfortable reality, in which monetary policy (their responsibility) and fiscal policy (the government's responsibility) overlap. Arguably, such is the case with the quantitative easing policies that began in response to the Global Financial Crisis and that have subsequently proved to be totally addictive.[13] Chapter 3 explains more.

Rules of thumb

Admittedly, it's possible to find central bankers willing to rise above the political fray. Even then, however, there's no guarantee of price stability. Reflecting on the 1970s economic experience – a 'stagflationary' period, during which both unemployment and inflation were too high simultaneously – Bernanke observed that:

First, during this period, central bankers seemed to have been excessively optimistic about the ability of activist monetary policies to offset shocks to output and to deliver permanently low levels of unemployment. Second, monetary policymakers appeared to underestimate their own contributions to the inflationary problems of the time, believing instead that inflation was in large part the result of nonmonetary forces ... [D]uring this period policymakers became more and more inclined to blame inflation on so-called cost-push shocks rather than on monetary forces. Cost-push shocks, in the paradigm of the time, included diverse factors such as union wage pressures, price increases by oligopolistic firms, and increases in the prices of commodities such as oil and beef brought about by adverse changes in supply conditions.[14]

Put simply, it's not just that economies evolve thanks to, for example, technological change, international competition and commodity price shocks. How we think about economies also evolves. That evolution, in turn, depends on our collective economic experience over periods of time. Most of us don't carry around in our heads a complex economic model full of mathematical equations. We use rules of thumb instead. Those rules, however, can change in response to a changing economic environment. As they do so, the task facing the average central banker becomes more challenging. Their own complex models break down, because those models implicitly assume our rules of thumb never change. If, however, we're collectively in the process of abandoning those rules, the central bankers' views about the economy – based upon the constancy of those rules – become increasingly inaccurate.

Back in the 1970s, the typical policymaker's objective was to minimise unemployment. Superficially, it was a perfectly reasonable objective. How could anyone argue with the idea that unemployment should be as low as possible? The message, however, was clear: central banks would not respond to increases in inflation, both because doing so would threaten the labour market objective and because inflation was typically regarded as a 'non-monetary event', a result of bad luck rather than bad judgement. Delivering price stability was simply not an aim of macroeconomic policy.

The approach created an inflationary free for all. For companies, the message was simple: raise prices as far as you can, and pass on cost increases as quickly as you can. For workers, particularly those belonging to powerful unions, the message was equally transparent: your job is effectively guaranteed by the government, so demand whatever wage increase you can get away with. When policymakers did respond, it was typically by imposing price and incomes restraints. Yet, if inflation was already distorting the invisible hand, these policies only made things worse. With markets unable to function properly, attempts to squash inflation only led to greater inefficiency, lower growth and, with it, higher unemployment.

Gradualism has to cut both ways

Fast forward to the 2020s and a similar challenge materialised. The years following the Global Financial Crisis were characterised by too little, rather than too much, inflation. Central bankers genuinely began to believe that the years of high inflation were receding further and further into the past. Their explanation for this apparent success was simple: in effect, success bred success. The longer inflation remained low, the more the public believed it would remain low. In central banking language, monetary policies were totally credible. Only the smallest of interest-rate adjustments would be needed because, every time the central bank acted, the public would fully understand the central bank's intentions and, as such, would adjust their own expectations accordingly. In this world, demanding an inflation-busting pay increase would be pointless, for the simple reason that inflation was, in effect, dead and buried.

To be fair, not all central bankers reached this rather complacent conclusion. As Isabel Schnabel, a member of the European Central Bank's (ECB) Executive Board, noted in May 2022:

> The fact that inflation is, to a considerable extent, driven by global factors does not mean that monetary policy can or should remain on the sidelines. On the contrary, persistent global shocks imply that the firm anchoring of inflation expectations has become more important than ever.
>
> And as risks are growing that current high inflation is becoming entrenched in expectations, the urgency for monetary policy to take action to protect price stability has increased in recent weeks.[15]

Others at the ECB, however, advised caution, arguing in favour of 'gradualism', given the enormous uncertainties confronting the global economy in the wake of pandemic-related lockdowns and the ongoing impact on both inflation and real incomes of Russia's invasion of Ukraine. According to Fabio Panetta, another member of the ECB's Executive Board:

> . . . gradualism is necessary when the transmission of policy changes to the economy is uncertain. In such conditions, the optimal policy involves moving cautiously and observing how the economy responds to a gradual adjustment.[16]

Panetta's call for gradualism was based on three reasons: the uncertain scale of negative supply shocks; the absence of any obvious precedent to learn from; and the extent to which more aggressive tightening of monetary policy could trigger undesirable volatility in financial markets. Still, Panetta accepted that gradualism might need to be abandoned if inflationary expectations were to shift decisively higher.

The logic of gradualism in the face of uncertainty is based on a seminal paper by William Brainard, published in 1967.[17] One of Brainard's key points was simply that shifting policy aggressively in a fast-changing world might have unexpected – and possibly undesirable – side effects. In other words, even if changes in policy were intended to make the world a better place, they might suffer from the law of unintended (and, perhaps, misunderstood) consequences. Honest attempts to reduce unemployment rates in the 1970s through a variety of stimulus measures misfired, because policymakers failed to recognise that inflation was already spiralling out of control.

This argument, however, must surely cut both ways. Uncertainty is always with us. It's true that the Russian invasion of Ukraine had huge effects on global energy and food prices; but those effects might have happened earlier had the West imposed more severe sanctions following Russia's invasion of Georgia in 2008 or its annexation of Crimea in 2014. Equally, while the Covid-19 pandemic proved to be devastating in both human and economic terms, Covid wasn't the first virus the 'modern world' has had to grapple with: from the cholera pandemics of the nineteenth century through to the 1918–1921 Spanish flu, and from the Asian and Hong Kong flus of the 1950s and 1960s through to the outbreak of severe acute respiratory syndrome (SARS) in 2003, each offered lessons for the present day.

We falsely attribute patterns to our own skills and abilities

The problem is not so much that the world has become more uncertain – how can it have, when the future at any point in time is unknowable? – but, rather, that central bankers somehow thought they were operating for many years in a world of greater certainty, underpinned by their own monetary architecture. The evidence in their favour was the idea of sustainably lower inflation and, with it, sustainably lower interest rates; but the fact that such results were maintained for many years said little about whether such conditions might continue into an (uncertain) future.

To understand why, consider a repeated coin toss. Assuming the coin has no intrinsic bias, we know that each toss has a 50 per cent chance of heads and an identical 50 per cent chance of tails. Knowing this, however, doesn't rule out the possibility that five repeated throws will all land heads up. Admittedly, the probability of such an event is low – only a little over 3 per cent; but it's not impossible. Yet were we to observe five repeated heads, we might begin to believe that the coin was biased. Our desire to extrapolate from those five tosses might be enough to persuade ourselves that the coin was more likely to come up heads on the sixth toss. We would, of course, be wrong.

To a degree, the same applies to periods of apparent economic calm. We begin to believe that nothing can go wrong. We lose sight of past upheavals. We cannot help but believe that our policymakers have somehow 'taken charge'. Our own expectations – our 'rules of thumb' – adapt to our recent experience. Yet, as with the coin toss example, we can suddenly be given an abrupt wake up call, a shock of sobriety in which we belatedly recognise that the future is not always the same as the recent past. It was a lesson we should have learnt from the

Global Financial Crisis and any one of a number of financial upheavals in the 1980s and 1990s.

Back to Brainard. The key problem with a call for gradualism is that – if it applies at all – it should apply in all circumstances, and not simply in those which *appear* more uncertain. Yet there was nothing 'gradualistic' about the monetary policies on offer after the Global Financial Crisis. Interest rates were slashed to zero (and eventually below zero); quantitative easing became a constant companion, when originally it was only intended to be an 'emergency' monetary measure; and ahead of the pandemic, the Federal Reserve shifted towards an 'asymmetric' inflation target, in which inflationary overshoots would be encouraged as a counterweight to past inflationary undershoots. It was as if the only possible threat came from deflation, not inflation. Central bankers placed all their chips on red, thinking that there was only one game in town. When inflation made an unexpected reappearance during the pandemic, it proved near enough impossible for central bankers to reconsider the available evidence and respond swiftly enough to a new – yet also startlingly familiar – threat.

Compounding their errors

In truth, central bankers compounded their seemingly dismissive attitude towards uncertainty in three distinct ways. First, in the years following the Global Financial Crisis, they began to offer 'forward guidance'. The idea was to provide an indication to anyone who cared to listen – with a particular nod to those operating in financial markets – as to where policy rates might be heading in coming months and years. At the time, central bankers wanted to discourage investors from believing that interest rates would automatically rise in response to evidence of rebounding economic activity, worrying that such perceived tightening would stop any recovery in its tracks. In effect, they were claiming that somehow they were better informed – and in fact more confident – about the future than the millions of people involved in financial markets and the broader economy. It's difficult to see why this might have been the case. Subsequent events only served to disabuse central banks of the notion: after all, they failed to foresee the surge in inflation beginning in 2021.

Second, central bankers offered inflation forecasts that always justified their existing monetary stance. Their view of the future offered inflationary perfection. In two years' time, they were always able to hit their mandated target. Policy today was always precisely calibrated to ensure that there would be inflationary success tomorrow. Admittedly, the route towards this inflationary nirvana was sometimes a little bumpy and forecast 'ranges' suggested there was some uncertainty along the way; but for the most part, central bankers were confident in their ability to deliver what was being asked of them.

Third, central bankers began to believe their own propaganda, in effect arguing that their own anti-inflation credibility more or less guaranteed that inflation expectations would remain well behaved. They were, in effect, second-guessing the public's reaction to any inflationary shock. Put simply, the public's existing rules of thumb would not be abandoned, no matter the degree of inflationary provocation, because the public's faith in the central banking priesthood was unwavering. In this theological universe, it was simply impossible for inflation to pick up. Central bankers, it seemed, had spent too much of their time listening to Professor Pangloss,[18] willing to believe that, yes, all is for the best in the best of all possible worlds.

At the time of writing, this optimism appears to be especially unfortunate. With inflation rates having hit levels not seen in four or five decades, yet with interest rates increasing only reluctantly in response, central bankers are in danger of treating the public as naive, hoping they will blindly accept whatever the policymakers want them to believe. As the remainder of this book demonstrates, however, the successful control of inflation is not merely a technical exercise in which interest rates are adjusted like thermostats on the living-room wall. It is also, importantly, an outcome that depends on the public's willingness to maintain rules of thumb in the face of severe economic and financial adversity. Once those rules of thumb are abandoned, there's every risk of an economic and financial free for all, in which political and social dislocations become ever more visible. In those circumstances, a technocratic central bank is in danger of losing public support, making the pursuit of price stability doubly hard.

At this point, it's worth exploring inflation's long and undistinguished history. Doing so reminds us that inflation often reappears unexpectedly. Worse, inflation can sometimes be engineered by leaders who would rather have the printing presses do the dirty work that, in other circumstances, would be the task of fiscal policy.

2

A History of Inflation, Money and Ideas

Roman inflation – the sixteenth-century 'price revolution' – the emergence of the quantity theory – Friedman exonerated – the French revolution re-examined – China's three-way inflation shock – the end of the gold standard – understanding the Great Moderation – the inflationary bias against deflation

Inflation may have many causes, but ultimately it is a story that can be described in one of two ways. Either inflation reflects rising prices of most things (goods, services, wages, profits, rents), or instead it reflects the falling value of money. These two perspectives are, in truth, two sides of the same coin.

Money's slippery history

Money's role in society has typically been seen as (i) a medium of exchange (a mechanism to avoid the inefficiencies of barter); (ii) a store of value; and (iii) a unit of account. Inflation makes money's role as a unit of account especially slippery. It's as if the measurements on a 12-inch (or 30cm) ruler gradually become smaller and smaller over time. The true length of the ruler never changes, but the 'measured' length shifts from, say, 12 inches to 16 inches to 20 inches.

Inflation also, however, potentially affects money's role as both a medium of exchange and a store of value. People won't accept money as a medium of exchange if, say, a dollar bill threatens to buy a lot less tomorrow than it can buy today. People won't save money if they fear its value will erode over time: like the Turkish washing machine hoarder, they'll find another way to preserve their wealth.

A further complication is that not all money is the same. One person's inflationary (or indeed, deflationary) experience may not match another's.

The Roman angle

The distinction between different forms of money has mattered throughout history. Holders of *denarii* in the third-century CE Roman Empire would have experienced a massive loss of purchasing power. Over an extended period, the silver content in a typical *denarius* fell from around 90 per cent to only 5 per cent. Admittedly, the gold *aureus* also lost value, but the decline was much more modest: a Diocletian *aureus* had a little over half of the gold content of a similar coin minted at the time of Julius Caesar, three centuries earlier.

The 'exchange rate' between these two coins – one nominally silver, one gold – inevitably shifted hugely over the centuries. When the *aureus* was first created, it was worth 25 *denarii*. Three hundred years later, when Constantine replaced the *aureus* with the *solidus*, the new gold coin was worth 275,000 *denarii*.

Poorer members of Roman society were unlikely to have been paid in *aurei* and would hardly have been able to accumulate sufficient *denarii* to swap their rapidly debasing silver coins into more reliable gold ones. Put another way, the inflation suffered in Roman society in the 'long' third century CE – with estimates suggesting an overall increase in the price level of approaching 20,000 per cent over a 150-year period[1] – was felt most obviously by the poor, not the rich.[2]

The 'price revolution' – more a 'price creep'

From the late fifteenth century through to the early seventeenth, the world was subject to what subsequently became known as the 'price revolution'. By today's standards, not a great deal happened price-wise: in Spain, the epicentre of the 'revolution', prices rose 315 per cent, the equivalent of 1.4 per cent per year (and thus, below today's typical inflation targets). Other countries also saw sustained price increases. An English pound at the beginning of the sixteenth century was worth only 25 pence (using modern denominations) a hundred years later.

Nevertheless, as Figure 2.1 suggests, the price revolution was still an unusual event, judged both by what had happened previously and what occurred subsequently. For much of pre-industrial history, prices both rose and fell, but rarely moved in either direction sustainably. What went up typically came back down (and vice versa). In that respect, the long sixteenth century was revolutionary. Explanations for this sustained loss of monetary value vary. Some argue that the apparent loss was no more than an illusion, a reflection of demographic changes that drove up the recorded prices of basic foodstuffs (everyone needs food, after all), leaving less money available to spend on manufactured goods. By implication, rising food prices were offset by falling non-food prices. As many manufactured goods prices went unrecorded, however, this is at best a matter of conjecture, rather than a fully tested hypothesis.

A second explanation – inspired by, for example, Henry VIII's reign in England – relies on observed debasement of the coinage. Keen to fund wars and live a life of relative opulence, Henry secretly stockpiled a vast number of newly minted coins with reduced gold and silver content. Later, when faced with a bullion shortage, he released the debased coins – with some 'silver' coins no more than silver-plated copper coins – into the economy. His decision – once discovered – led to the withdrawal of 'good' coins from the system and, almost inevitably, a period of steadily rising prices, a fine example of Gresham's law, in which 'bad money drives out good'. Yet such behaviour was typically nation specific, so cannot easily account for the widespread nature of the 'revolution'.

A third explanation is simply that the late fifteenth century and much of the sixteenth witnessed a huge expansion of silver

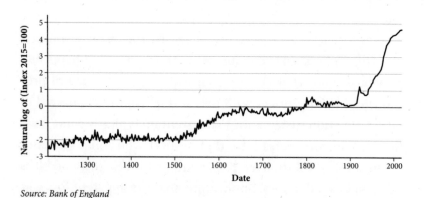

Source: Bank of England

Figure 2.1: The price level rose consistently between 1500 and 1650 in the UK during the 'price revolution'

supplies and, hence, of money supply. The process began in central Europe, where new silver discoveries and more productive techniques led to increased output in the likes of Bohemia and Hungary. The biggest part of the revolution, however, stemmed from the activities of Spanish *conquistadors* – and, in time, their colonial European rivals – in the Americas. These violent adventurers exploited a combination of huge silver reserves, notably in Peru's Potosi mine, and Andean mercury deposits, a vital ingredient in the production of silver.[3] One consequence was a huge increase in Spanish purchasing power, which in turn triggered a large increase in the import of fripperies from the rest of Europe. The resulting Spanish balance of payments current account deficit was funded through a continuous outflow of silver (easy enough to deliver, given that Potosi was, in effect, a giant silver 'printing press'), which in turn increased the volume of money supply elsewhere in Europe.

The consequences of this exchange were far-reaching. Once the silver supplies were established, the Spanish themselves didn't have to work too hard. Like today's oil producers, they could simply live off what was being dug out of the ground (mostly, in the *conquistadors'* case, the work of their slaves). This, arguably, marked the beginning of a slow end to what had been a formidable empire. As producers in other nations – the English and Dutch among them – competed for Spain's favour, they became more skilled at manufacturing (weapons, among other things) than the Spanish themselves. And as silver lost some of its magical lustre, reflected in a continuous increase in prices, so Spain's imperial and economic ambitions began to wane. Money doesn't always guarantee lasting riches.

The beginning of the quantity theory

Perhaps not surprisingly, these experiences gave rise to new thinking about the relationship between money and prices. In the first half of the sixteenth century, inflationary problems in Prussia and Poland led to the emergence of ideas that today would be regarded as some of the earliest thinking regarding the so-called quantity theory of money.[4] In 1517, Nicholas Copernicus – he of heliocentric fame – stated that:

> Money can lose its value also through excessive abundance, if so much silver is coined as to heighten people's desire for silver bullion. For in this way the coinage's estimation vanishes when it cannot buy as much silver as the money itself contains, and then I find greater advantage in destroying the coin by melting the silver. The solution is to mint no more coinage until it recovers its par value.

Although it's tempting to think that Copernicus was expressing a view linking the quantity of money to prices, on closer inspection his argument relates only to a specific price. He was worried that the excessive minting of coins would reduce their value relative to the value of silver contained within those coins, and thus it made sense under those circumstances to melt down the coins to extract the silver (a modern-day equivalent might be the theft of catalytic converters from cars in a bid to extract platinum, palladium or rhodium).[5] There was no reference whatsoever to prices more generally, and no reference to any kind of price index linked to a basket of goods and services. Indeed, it's doubtful that the concept of a 'price level' even existed at that point.

It didn't take long, however, for the concept to be established, even if it was in the most rudimentary of forms. In 1542, one Peter Kmita, the palatine of Cracow, wrote to Duke Albert of Prussia offering the following observation:

> ... the value or worth of every common thing (not to name them all) is raised excessively. But as for the reason, nobody is so foolish as not to see that the multitude of coins is to blame, which is in no relation to either the gulden[6] [a gold coin] or the things to be bought, as it used to be in former times.

As Thomas Levenson notes, in mid-seventeenth-century England, attempts to deal with debasement, counterfeiting and coin clipping led to the development of advanced coin presses.[7] In 1662, the Royal Mint created a new production line making coins with embellished rims and deeply embossed designs on front and rear. The intricate rims made 'clipping' a less than useful exercise, while the sophisticated imagery was difficult to replicate. Yet old coinage – some of which went back a good two hundred years – continued to circulate alongside the new. And because anyone with even the tiniest amount of financial sophistication knew the old coinage – clipped, counterfeited, debased – was not as trustworthy as the new, it was the new that was squirrelled away, in effect leading to a divorce between money's role as a medium of exchange and as a store of value. Typically, only the better off were able to stockpile the new coins. In contrast, the poor were left more exposed to the potential rejection of the old, unreliable coins.

The new coins were, in some ways, too good to be true. Their silver content was worth more in terms of gold in Paris than in London. Illegal though it may have been, the new coins were melted down and smuggled across the Channel. In Paris, the resulting silver contraband was swapped into gold. Shipped back to England, this gold was then used for the purchase of more of the new coins. So long as the arbitrage opportunity existed, the process continued. In effect, the Royal Mint's new coins were rapidly vanishing, leaving England stuck with old coins that were, as before, vulnerable to clipping and counterfeiting.

Locke versus Newton

This, in turn, led to a debate between two of England's foremost thinkers about the nature of money. John Locke (1632–1704) insisted that silver's value – and hence, money's value – was fixed for all time by convention, the equivalent of arguing that the length of a 12-inch ruler was handed down by neverchanging sovereign edict (or, to the extent that monarchs were extensions of divine rule, by God). He based this on the idea that silver was 'natural', and thus ought not be subject to the laws of supply and demand determining prices elsewhere. In that sense, silver was at the centre of the economic and financial universe, in the same way as the sun was at the centre of the solar system.[8]

Sir Isaac Newton (1643–1727) – now earning his own mint at the Royal Mint, having already dealt with gravity, the rules of the physical universe and calculus – claimed instead that money (and silver, its primary component) was just like any other commodity, and thus subject to the laws of supply and demand. In his view, two reforms were required to solve England's monetary mess. First, abolish all the old coins, so that the incentive to hoard (or melt down) the new coins was removed. Second, adjust the value of silver coins with respect to the value of gold, so that any arbitrage opportunity (particularly between London and Paris) was removed.

It's tempting to conclude that Newton's view is much more 'modern' than Locke's. After all, foreign exchange markets offer continuous live prices, reflecting changes in the demand for, and supply of, currencies. Yet, in some ways, Locke's view lives on. What, after all, does credible inflation targeting claim, other than to allow the value of a currency to decline at a predictable yet insignificant rate year by year? Is that so different from Locke's claim that the value of a currency is dictated by nature or, for the religiously inclined, divine providence? The only real difference lies in who 'safeguards' the value of the currency. In Locke's day, it was God and the monarch, represented by an embossed sovereign image on the coins in question. Today, it is the central bank, sometimes (but not always) reflecting parliamentary edict.

Locke and Newton weren't the only brilliant minds debating the nature of money and prices. Jean Bodin (1530–1596), the French social philosopher, had already argued that an influx of Spanish silver from the New World was the primary cause of rising European commodity prices. Locke himself went on to declare that the price level was always proportional to the money supply (however defined). David Hume (1711–1776), the great Scottish philosopher and 'cause and effect' pioneer, perhaps not surprisingly imposed causality on the relationship, claiming that changes in the stock of money caused changes in prices, not the reverse. Hume also argued that the causal relationship was far from instantaneous, introducing what today would be described as 'money illusion'. In Hume's view, some groups were simply better placed than others to observe rising price pressures. Businesses, for example, might be quicker than their workers to spot higher prices, allowing them to boost profits in the short term, even as, in real terms, household incomes were squeezed. In the long term, however, such illusions – at least according to Hume – would disappear. Mere money could not permanently change economic destinies.

It's important to recognise, however, that these were arguments mostly made from first principles. There was little in the way of empirical testing, for the simple reason that there were hardly any data. The data that did exist typically related to a currency's value versus gold (or, for that matter, other currencies). Nevertheless, when a monetary shock did take place, those in favour of the fledging quantity theory were quick to claim victory. Such was the case with the Bullionist Controversy triggered by the UK's decision in 1797 to sever the pound's link to gold.

In truth, there was little choice: the rising costs of the Napoleonic Wars had drained the Bank of England's gold reserves to such an extent that convertibility of sterling into gold could no longer be guaranteed. David Ricardo (1772–1823) and others argued – from first principles – that the Bank of England's policies had most definitely created inflation. Their case was simple enough. The loss of convertibility into gold meant that the bank was now free to issue as much 'paper' money as it wished. The resulting increase in money supply raised domestic prices and, moreover, lowered the value of sterling – now in more abundant supply – relative to gold.

These conclusions, however, were based on the flimsiest of hard evidence. The increase in domestic prices relative to foreign prices, for example, was no more than an assumption, for the simple reason that no one in those days was in the business of compiling price indices.

As time went on, however, the quantity theory was finessed, resulting in the now famous equation of exchange (or, for its critics, the now infamous identity of the tautologically obvious), developed by Irving Fisher (1867–1947):

$$MV=PT$$

(or, for its critics, $MV \equiv PT$, in other words MV is tautologically identical to PT)

where M is the stock of money, V is its velocity of circulation
(the number of times it changes hands in, say, a year), P is the
price level and T is the volume of transactions.[9]

Advocates of this formulation made a number of key claims:
(i) prices moved in proportion to changes in money supply; (ii)
the direction of causation ran from money to prices, not the
other way round; (iii) real economic variables were determined
by real things – demographics, technological change, human
capital – with changes in the stock of money ultimately having
no lasting effect on economic activity; and (iv) money supply
was, in effect, an exogenous variable, controlled by the issuing
authority, whether it be a mint, a central bank, a government
or, for that matter, a Peruvian silver mine.[10]

None of these claims is necessarily unreasonable. Yet none
of them can be derived from Fisher's equation. The assembled
letters are no more than an accounting identity. Causality must
be imposed, as must definitions. For example, not everyone
agrees that the sixteenth-century price revolution resulted
from rising M: an alternative view is that much of the increase
in prices was a reflection of rising V, itself a consequence of the
impact on money demand of urbanisation and occupational
specialisation in major European countries, thus creating more
frequent opportunities for economic exchange.[11]

Keynes and the quantity theorists

John Maynard Keynes (1883–1946) was one of those who
objected to the claims of quantity theorists. Understandably, he

wasn't keen on the idea that the 'real economy' was a given, determined by a mixture of long-term 'supply-side' factors that had no room for depression-era levels of unemployment. Keynes felt that, in a depression economy, policy stimulus – in the form of more M or, via increased public spending, more T – would have a bigger effect on output and employment than prices. And Keynes suspected that V would automatically adjust to changes in other variables, so that the supposedly stable (or at least predictable) relationship between M and P was no more than a figment of the imagination. Interestingly, much the same debate took place in the immediate aftermath of the 2008 Global Financial Crisis, when strict monetarists – the intellectual offspring of earlier quantity theorists – argued erroneously that the 'printing' of money associated with quantitative easing would quickly result in excessive inflation: they ignored the fact that the creation of what might best be described as 'public' money only served to offset the destruction of 'private' money in the form of hitherto liquid collateralised debt obligations and their ilk.[12] As for the Great Depression's causes, didn't the Wall Street Crash prove that there had been a collapse in business confidence – so-called 'animal spirits' – thanks to the perceived disappearance of investment opportunities, unleashing a downward multiplier that could only be reversed through, say, a sizeable dose of fiscal stimulus? What additional role, if any, could money play?[13]

Friedman fights back

In the decades in the immediate aftermath of the Second World War, it was easy enough to conclude – as Milton Friedman (1912–2006) did in 1965, with tongue firmly in cheek – that 'we are all Keynesians now'. Yet, as inflation bubbled up in the late 1960s, the quantity theorists hit back, supported by a new empiricism built, most obviously, on Friedman's and Anna Schwartz's (1915–2012) monumental *A Monetary History of the United States, 1867–1960.*[14] Friedman, Schwartz and their followers established four key points: (i) the Great Depression, associated with collapsing output *and* prices, was a consequence of a huge monetary contraction, helped along by multiple bank failures; (ii) had the Federal Reserve printed money, there was every chance that some of that contraction would have been avoided; (iii) the available evidence suggested that, although the relationship between money and prices was not stable, it was both predictable and causal, at least over the medium term; and (iv) the existence of long and variable lags meant that economic 'fine tuning' of the kind typically favoured by policy-makers in the 1950s and 1960s was ultimately self-defeating.[15] Friedman's arguments in effect changed perceptions of histor-ical reality, even if the focus on money diverted attention away from other important factors, notably multiple bank failures.[16] At a conference in 2002 to mark Friedman's ninetieth birthday, Ben Bernanke concluded with the following heartfelt words:

> Let me end my talk by abusing slightly my status as an official representative of the Federal Reserve. I would like to say to Milton and Anna: Regarding the Great Depression. You're right, we did it. We're very sorry. But thanks to you, we won't do it again.[17]

And, of course, the acknowledgement of the Federal Reserve's past errors was also an indirect reason for the slashing of interest rates and the adoption of quantitative-easing policies during the Global Financial Crisis. The Federal Reserve was not about to be blamed for causing a Great Depression Mk II.

Rewriting history: quantitative fiction, revolutionary reality

Friedman's success in re-establishing aspects of the quantity theory allowed others to delve back into history, assembling price indices sometimes from the scantiest of data.[18] Suddenly, it was possible – so it seemed – to explain inflations great and small through monetary influences of one kind or another. Each episode could be blamed on the foolishness or greed of the monetary and fiscal authorities.

One such re-examined episode – inevitably – is the French Revolution. On one measure, prices rose by a total of 26,566.7 per cent between February 1790 and February 1796, translating into an average annual inflation rate of 150.6 per cent.[19] Yet this 'fact' depends on a particular interpretation of events in the 1790s which, on closer scrutiny, reveals that the relationship between money and prices is far more complicated than monetarists typically are willing to concede.[20]

At the heart of the issue is a fundamental question. Specifically, what counts as money? Prior to the revolution, money was a mixture of the formal, in the shape of officially embossed but privately issued coins (anyone with a spare silver bowl was welcome to pop along to the local mint and have it melted down into coins) and the informal, such as bills of exchange and other assorted 'unofficial' credits.

With the onset of revolution, however, the newly formed National Assembly encountered a serious problem. On the one hand, it wanted to declare many existing taxes illegal (and even if it hadn't, revolutionary fervour up and down the country would have led to non-compliance in tax payments). On the other hand, it was keen to honour the state's debts. For all the sense of a new beginning, there was no desire to default. Those who had lent to the state had, one way or another, to be paid back in full.[21] Worse, with revolution afoot, few new lenders were forthcoming. Meanwhile, with no one sure of the legal status of loans, whether private or public, those that had money in the form of coins understandably hoarded them. In Fisher terms, the velocity of circulation of money collapsed. And so, eventually, did the economy.

One way around this – remarkably similar in spirit to modern-day quantitative easing – was to organise an injection of new money. Making new coins was more or less impossible, particularly since anyone able to spirit their precious metal out of the country did exactly that. Yet the issuance of the first *assignats* in 1789 suggested that they were more bills of exchange than money, pieces of paper that paid interest, backed by lands seized from the Catholic Church. Only later, as the hoarding of coins continued, were non-interest-bearing 'money-*assignats*' created. Even so, they were conceptually odd, offering liquidity based on land, that most illiquid of assets.[22]

Beyond their conceptual oddness, they were initially also produced only in relatively high denominations – the equivalent of discovering today that a US$1,000 bill is the smallest 'legal tender'. One consequence was the production of smaller-denomination *billets de confiance* by local trusted institutions, including town halls and reputable manufacturers. This process was designed to deal better with a cash shortage that otherwise imposed a bigger burden on the poor – who could hardly be paid in large denomination notes, and certainly couldn't buy anything with those notes – than the rich.

Yet as *assignats* and *billets de confiance* spread through communities, a significant problem arose. Although, if caught, the penalty for it was death, counterfeiting became a very attractive 'get-rich-quick' scheme. And as there was no easy way to spot the difference between a real *assignat* and a fake, and as *billets de confiance* were being produced by all and sundry, it didn't take long before people began to lose confidence in the new, revolutionary, monetary regime. Transactions would take place only in conditions of mutual trust. And, as trust evaporated, so transactions fell. Retailers would increasingly refuse to sell their produce, believing that they were better off stockpiling what they already had than stockpiling what might prove to be totally worthless paper. Printing more 'money' in these circumstances only made matters worse, leading to huge price increases, the further hoarding of coins and, inevitably, a collapse in the revolutionary exchange rate, making imports prohibitively expensive.

As Rebecca Spang memorably writes in *Stuff and Money in the Time of the French Revolution*:

> Contemporary economists often treat the past as if it were the present in fancy dress, as if the only questions worth asking about it concerned the reliability of available numerical data.[23]

Yet it's abundantly clear that late-eighteenth-century perceptions of money differed hugely from the apparent simplicity – perhaps even naivety – of the quantity theory, particularly as encapsulated in the Fisher equation. What is, and isn't, regarded as money is not simply a matter of state decree. It is also a reflection of social mores and customs, notably the extent to which any medium of exchange can enjoy widespread and continued trust. Over two hundred years later, the role of trust was, once again, centre stage. During the Global Financial Crisis, banks – the institutions at the heart of the financial system – stopped trusting each other. Rising interbank rates pointed to a form of wholesale money hoarding, the equivalent of the coin hoarding witnessed in revolutionary France. Central banks had no choice but to step in, otherwise the loss of confidence in what might loosely be termed 'near money' threatened a terrifying collapse in final demand.

China's hyperinflation

Even when state decrees do play a part, public perceptions can still be of the utmost importance. Such was the case in China between 1937 and 1949, from the Japanese invasion to the eventual triumph of Mao Zedong's Communists. A single nation was, in effect, divided up to be ruled over by three warring governments, each of which issued its own currency (or currencies) – a move that subsequently led to outright currency wars.[24] The Japanese banned those living in the Chinese territories it had occupied from using Nationalist currency. The Nationalists and Communists responded in kind. Legal trade between the divided parts of the nation became nigh impossible.

Illegal trade, however, could still be financed, leading to all sorts of financial shenanigans. Most obviously, Nationalist currency seized by the Japanese in the newly occupied territories was 'illegally' used to buy merchandise from Nationalist territories, where Nationalist currency was still legal tender, in effect flooding those territories with excess cash. Alongside the costs of pursuing the war and the inability easily to raise funds at reasonable interest rates, the inevitable result was a rapid rise in inflation within those territories.

Initially, however, the rise was less a consequence of monetary expansion and more a result of rapidly rising velocity: with growing inflationary fears, people simply wanted to get rid of cash. Put another way, the rise in inflation reflected a collapse in trust on behalf of the public. Preserving wealth under these circumstances led to an 'anything but cash' attitude.

Money matters, and so does trust

Each of these historical episodes – from ancient Rome to the Peruvian silver mines, and from the French Revolution through to China's three-way split – suggests, firstly, that money absolutely does matter (in that sense, monetarists can breathe a sigh of relief); but secondly, it also suggests that our attitudes towards money matter, too. Inflation isn't just caused by the printing press: it can also be a consequence of a breakdown of trust. Monetary and fiscal authorities lose the trust of the people. People stop trusting each other. Institutions refuse to lend to each other. The important consequence of this observation is that the printing of money is far more consequential on some occasions than on others. In that sense, the quantity theory is too simplistic, its success dependent on what, precisely, is influencing the velocity of circulation (or the desire to hoard money, rather than spend it).

A general historical proof of these two propositions comes from a closer look at economic experience over the last hundred years or so. The mechanisms that, for the most part, anchored the supply of money and, indirectly, the price level were mostly abandoned in the twentieth century. Historically, money in its various forms was tied to the supply of precious metal. There were obvious exceptions – the aforementioned *assignats* and, during the American Civil War, Confederate dollars that ultimately proved worthless (see chapter 3) – but before the twentieth century, money and precious metals were mostly joined at the hip.

Sometimes, this connection produced perverse results. In the late nineteenth century, many countries experienced deflation, due to the impact on economic growth of the Industrial Revolution. Put simply, with T rising faster than before and M effectively constrained by the limited supply of gold and silver, either V had to rise or P had to fall. In the event, prices fell. This was, in effect, a good deflation: prices fell relative to both wages and profits. In other words, 'real' incomes rose. A rapid increase in productivity (thanks in part to the economies of scale associated with the growth of mass markets) led to a hitherto unimaginable surge in the volume of production. The mass markets, in turn, reflected the spread of railways and ocean-going freight. Sheffield steelmakers, for example, could suddenly sell their products all over the world.

For the most part, however – and with the obvious exception of the 'long' sixteenth-century price revolution – the link to precious metal, formalised in the nineteenth century in terms of the gold standard – kept money 'sound'. Only when that link was broken, such as with the UK's decision temporarily to sever ties with gold in the Napoleonic era, did price instability reappear.

The end of metallic money

Yet, in the early decades of the twentieth century, a system that had worked almost by accident – or, more charitably, by convention – completely fell apart. Admittedly, it didn't happen all at once, but the inflationary costs of the First World War led most countries temporarily to suspend membership of the gold standard. In the 1920s, governments had to decide whether to return to the system at the pre-war parity or, instead, to devalue. The French devalued. The British – at the insistence of Winston Churchill, the then-chancellor of the Exchequer – decided to return to the pre-war parity. It was an immensely costly decision, earning a stinging rebuke from John Maynard Keynes, who famously described the gold standard as a 'barbarous relic'.[25]

The problem was simple: because British prices had risen so much during the war and its aftermath, returning the UK to the gold standard at the pre-war parity meant that, in foreign currency terms, British prices were far too high, making British exports uncompetitive and, by the same token, foreign imports absurdly cheap. The only way of dealing with the problem was to impose austerity on the British economy in a bid to drive domestic prices and wages lower, thus making British exports cheaper in foreign terms. The General Strike – indirectly, an act of resistance – followed in 1926. Thereafter, persistent fears of sterling devaluation led to an exodus of gold to the other side of the Atlantic, forcing interest rates in the US down to lower and lower levels – a process which, in turn, contributed to the stock-market bubble that ended with the 1929 Wall Street Crash. Two years later, with the onset of the Great Depression, the UK left the gold standard altogether, prompting Sidney Webb, a minister hailing from the 1929–1931 minority Labour government, to say 'nobody told us we could do that'. Others followed later that decade: the Americans in 1933 and the French in 1936. Those quickest to leave were able to offer monetary support earliest, enabling them to escape from the effects of depression quicker than others. Their relative success ultimately doomed the gold standard to the dustbin of history.[26]

Thereafter, the relationship between money, prices and the broader economy changed fundamentally. Table 2.1 shows the degree to which a British pound at the beginning of each century since the reign of Edward I changed over the next hundred years.[27] If (and it's quite a big 'if') historic aggregate price data are in any way a reflection of reality, the table highlights the impact of the price revolution, the American and

Table 2.1: The value of 'British' money: what £1 was worth 100 years later

1300	1400	1500	1600	1700	1800	1900	2000
£1.00→	£0.99						
	£1.00→	£1.11					
		£1.00→	£0.25				
			£1.00→	£0.71			
				£1.00→	£0.46		
					£1.00→	£1.49	
						£1.00→	£0.02

Source: Bank of England, author's calculations

French revolutions, the deflation of the late nineteenth century and, most glaringly, the inflation of the twentieth century. A pound issued in 1900 would be worth only two pence in 2000. Put another way, the twentieth century – and, for that matter, the first two decades of the twenty-first century – have witnessed more monetary destruction than any other period in economic history. And that's just in the UK, which, unlike Germany, Austria, Hungary and so many others, has never succumbed to hyperinflation.[28]

No one wants a falling price level any more

To be fair, the twentieth-century monetary loss amounts to a rather modest 4.3 per cent annual inflation rate. The key distinction between the last hundred years or so and earlier periods, however, is not so much the rate of inflation, as the absence of any serious deflation. Throughout history, the price level has both risen and fallen. During the twentieth century and beyond, price level declines have become rarities.[29] Indeed, as the twentieth century rolled into the twenty-first, the fear of price declines turned into something of a fetish. The possibility of 'good deflation', of the kind witnessed in the late nineteenth century, was ignored. Instead, all forms of deflation were regarded as economic developments best avoided.

To a degree, Keynes was responsible for this extreme aversion. If wages were 'sticky' and could not easily fall, then price declines would simply lead to collapsing profits and mass bankruptcies, threatening to deliver the mass unemployment seen in the 1930s. Other concerns related to the 'zero rate bound', in which 'real' interest rates would end up rising if deflation took hold, with interest rates on cash unable to fall below zero: under those circumstances, people would increasingly be incentivised to hoard cash, thereby adding further to deflationary woes. Finally, in a world in which both wages and prices were falling, the 'real' burden of existing debts would rise, threatening an increase in bankruptcies and, in turn, mass unemployment.

The Great Moderation: globalisation versus the wisdom of central banks

Inevitably, however, an approach that attempts to avoid deflation at all costs is likely to end up delivering an inflationary bias. Importantly, this bias will probably be in place even during periods when, arguably, 'good deflation' would have been perfectly acceptable. Such was the case during the time of the so-called Great Moderation, a period extending from the 1980s through to the Global Financial Crisis, during which a sustained spell of economic growth punctuated by only very modest recessions was accompanied by ever-lower and more stable inflation, at least when compared with the 1970s.

Although central bankers were keen to take the credit for this apparently successful period, the Great Moderation could be explained in other ways. Globalisation – notably the incorporation of low-cost producers, such as China and India, into the global trading system – led to a series of windfall gains for western consumers that were associated with, for example, cheaper clothing and lower-cost electronics. With manufactured goods prices falling relative to western incomes, 'real' incomes rose.

Central bankers could either allow prices overall to drift lower – threatening a persistent undershoot of their inflation targets – or instead, they could loosen monetary policy in a bid to force other prices higher, in order to offset the declines in manufactured goods prices. For the most part, they chose the latter, in effect forcing the prices of non-tradable services – and, for that matter, asset prices, such as equities and real estate – higher than they otherwise might have been. Put another way, even when 'good deflation' might have happened, policymakers made sure that it did not: indeed, such was the commitment to a particular inflation target 'at all times' that there really wasn't much scope for such flexibility.

An inflationary bias in times of deflation

This essentially meant that the policymakers' attitudes towards inflation were skewed. There were no circumstances in which deflation would be welcomed. If, as happened in the aftermath of the Global Financial Crisis, deflationary risks increased, policymakers would adopt an 'all-hands-on-deck' approach to limiting those risks. Knowing this, the public – and, for that matter, those involved in financial markets – would naturally begin to believe that interest rates would remain at historically low levels for ever more. Yet, by insisting that deflation would not be tolerated, central bankers were implicitly saying that they were, on balance, willing to tolerate more inflation. In 2020, that implicit view was made explicit when the Federal Reserve moved to an 'asymmetric' inflation target, by which it would happily allow inflation to run at above the 2 per cent 'central target' for extended periods of time.

The pandemic helped reinforce this bias. Faced with collapsing demand, central bankers naturally thought that, once again, economies were in danger of entering a deflationary downward spiral. Sticking to their usual approach, they offered interest-rate cuts (where they could) and quantitative easing. Yet the collapse in demand was hardly voluntary, and in no way represented the typical liquidation effects seen in a recession or (worse) a depression. Nor was there any recognition – other than through a vague discussion about long-run economic 'scarring' – of possible supply losses that, historically, had contributed to higher inflation. Bizarrely, when lockdowns ended and demand recovered, there was no rush to reverse the monetary stimulus, even though there was increasing evidence that, alongside rebounding demand, supply constraints – in other words, various forms of scarring – were proving to be unusually problematic. Inflation was the unfortunate result.

Reflections on history

Time for some conclusions. The monetarists and quantity theorists might not be completely right, but to their credit, they are right in very important ways. Money does matter. Too much of the stuff, offered too cheaply, can lead to inflation, irrespective of the 'starting conditions' or the 'credibility' of official institutions. Central banks and other policymakers ignore monetary growth at their peril. The Federal Reserve did nothing about the collapse in monetary growth in the early

1930s and, in consequence, turned what might have been a recession into the Great Depression. The fear of deflation in the early stages of the pandemic – a reflection of a significant bias in attitudes towards price stability – left monetary policy too loose for too long, and, in the US at least, monetary growth too strong. The roots of the post-pandemic rise in inflation lie in this world of monetary complacency, not in Russia's invasion of Ukraine in 2022 or China's ongoing Covid lockdowns.

Public and business attitudes towards money and inflation matter at least as much as the monetary conditions themselves. In some cases, this is obvious: for any given level of interest rates, for example, a collapsing stock market is nothing like as helpful to economic growth as a rising stock market. But in other cases, the situation is nowhere near as clear: did the issuers of *assignats* in the 1790s imagine that their new experimental currency would be so brutally rejected (partly because it lacked the secure backing of precious metal), triggering a monstrous loss of 'monetary' value? Could policymakers easily have foreseen the spike in wholesale funding rates during the Global Financial Crisis, a sign that our biggest financial institutions no longer trusted one another, each fearing excessive amounts of worthless 'near money' on others' balance sheets?

And what happens to public and business attitudes when, after decades of quiescent price pressures, inflation suddenly awakes from its slumbers? Do people happily believe the edicts uttered by the monetary authorities, as if they uniquely have the power to control inflation? Or, instead, do attitudes shift in ways that diminish the chances of bringing inflation quickly and easily under control?

Particularly in a world of fiat currencies, those policymakers who believe that inflation has been tamed are often too willing to ignore the historical evidence to the contrary. If there's anything to be learnt from the last hundred years – a period in which the value of money has fallen either slowly or rapidly, but has hardly ever risen – it is that policymakers are all too happy to believe that the recent past is a reliable guide to all our futures. It can be, but not always. The interaction between money and inflation is determined by how all of us behave, and not by the decisions made by central banking technocrats alone. Sometimes, our behaviour increases the chances of central bankers getting it wrong.

Now, however, it's time to think about the role of governments. Periods of inflation, it turns out, have more to do with our rulers – democratically elected or otherwise – than they would typically care to admit.

3

The Inflationary Role of Governments

Paying for the American Civil War – paying for the peace that followed – embracing inflation the Brazilian way – the fiscal arithmetic of inflation – Richard Burton and Elizabeth Taylor – the perils of quantitative easing – the ECB's determination to save the euro at any cost – the historical foolishness of Modern Monetary Theory

Uncivil war

S ome banknotes contain only the vaguest of promises regarding their true value, offering merely verbal relics from a bygone age. A modern polymer Bank of England £20 note includes the words 'I promise to pay the bearer on demand the sum of twenty pounds'. Historically, the bearer of such a note could pop down to the Bank of England and receive gold in exchange. That link, however, was severed in 1931, the year in which the UK left the gold standard. Since then, the Bank of

England's promise has been only loosely met in a series of – typically short-lived – commitments to currency stability, ranging from membership of the Bretton Woods exchange rate system through to money supply targets, shadowing of the Deutsche Mark, a brief sojourn in the Exchange Rate Mechanism of the European Monetary System and, since 1992, adherence to an inflation target. Yet, given how far the UK price level has risen over the last hundred years, it might be reasonable to conclude that the Bank of England's 'promise to pay' is a much weaker covenant than it once was, a reflection of the monetary freedom granted to a government no longer tied to the gold standard.

Admittedly, the pound sterling is not the currency it once was, losing value both domestically and on the foreign exchanges. The most successful currency of the last century or so is, of course, the US dollar, particularly in terms of its near-universal global acceptance (even if it, too, has lost value thanks to occasional inflationary ravages).

The dollar no longer bothers with promises – either current or defunct – regarding a link to gold.[1] It still, however, places its faith in God. The process started with the Coinage Act of 1864 – during the American Civil War – which authorised the treasury secretary to add the words 'In God We Trust' to lower-denomination coins. The following year, Congress passed a further bill – the last signed by Abraham Lincoln before his fatal encounter with John Wilkes Booth – allowing the inscription to become a feature of newly minted gold and silver coins.

Oddly, it took another nine decades before the magic words were added to paper currency. In 1955, Representative Charles E. Bennett of Florida introduced a resolution to the House requiring 'In God We Trust' to be added to all notes and coins. In a fit of nationalistic religious moralising, Bennett argued that 'while the sentiment of trust in God is universal and timeless, these particular four words ... are indigenous to our country'. As the Cold War was at its peak, he added for good measure: 'In these days when imperialistic and materialistic communism seeks to attack and destroy freedom, we should continually look for ways to strengthen the foundations of our freedom'.[2]

In hindsight, US dollars in the decades following the end of the American Civil War proved to be more trustworthy than anyone could possibly have imagined. During the war itself, the value of the federal dollar halved in relation to gold. In line with previous conflicts, it was far easier to finance a military build-up by issuing currency – raising prices, thus reducing 'real' incomes and, hence, real spending for typical workers – than resort to politically more contentious higher taxes or non-military expenditure cuts. Yet, between 1865 – the year in which the war ended – and 1879, all the dollar's wartime losses relative to gold were recouped. The worldwide gold shortage was already forcing prices lower in the US and elsewhere, as the volume of economic output rose more rapidly than before. In addition, however, Washington was terrified about facing another dose of inflation equivalent to that experienced during either the American Revolution or its slightly later French counterpart. Washington's fears, in turn, were stoked by the dominance of Northern financial interests over those in the South. Northern financiers had lent to Southern farmers. Falling prices increased the 'real' value of debt payments from South to North. The North thus got richer, even as the South became poorer. Restoring the pre-Civil War parity was a mechanism to ensure that the economic costs of the war were largely imposed on the former Confederate states.

Some pushed for an end to such deflationary policies. Prominent among them was William Jennings Bryan – 'you

shall not crucify mankind upon a cross of gold' – who advocated a return to a silver standard, which at a stroke would have
removed much of the deflationary impetus (silver's value relative to gold had fallen a long way). Yet Washington was really
in no mood to budge. It feared that the short-lived Confederacy
had been, among other things, a source of rampant inflation
and, thus, any move to 'print money' to help a defeated South
was simply a non-starter.

The Civil War had certainly led to terrible inflationary
outcomes across the Confederacy. Between the early months of
1861 and the end of the conflict, prices in the South rose ninety-
fold. Although partly a consequence of additional cash issuance,
printing money was not the only reason for the surge in
prices. Confidence in the currency collapsed remarkably quickly,
prompting those with Confederate dollars to rid themselves of
them as soon as they could. In other words, monetary velocity
went through the roof – a reflection of fears that the largely
agrarian South was no match economically for the industrialised
North. As one wizened Confederate soldier opined, 'Before the
war, I went to market with money in my pocket and brought
back my purchases in a basket: now I take my money in a basket
and bring home the things in my pocket.'[3]

Prices in the Confederacy rose twice as fast as wages, leading
inevitably to claims that greedy businesspeople were to blame.
Price ceilings were imposed, but, with the amount of money by
then sloshing around, these were about as useful as a Band-Aid
in fixing a leaking roof. Meanwhile, a Confederate soldier's
lot was not a happy one: in real terms, a typical soldier's pay
collapsed, so that, as the war drew to a close, he was likely to be
fighting for honour alone.

In the North, the dollar's pre-Civil War value was (eventually) restored, suggesting that 'In God We Trust' was a useful

shorthand for the preservation of monetary value over time, at least for creditors (Northern debtors may have been a little less enthusiastic). For those living in the Confederacy, however, the only visible monetary God was vengeful, destroying people's livelihoods – initially through the perils of inflation (eroding the real value of nominal wages) and later through the evils of deflation (increasing the real value of nominal debts). More than any other occasion, wartime proves that fiscal decisions made by government – whether to tax, to spend or to print – have a profound impact on prices, inflation and the distribution of income and wealth. 'In God We Trust', perhaps, but when it comes to government finances and inflation, trust is fragile indeed.

Printing money to make government finances look better

The factors that contribute to the sustainability or otherwise of government debt help explain why, sometimes, inflation is such an attractive option. In very simple terms, the change in the stock of government debt between one year and the next is determined by the interest paid on the existing stock of debt and the amount the government is borrowing to fund expenditure (excluding interest payments) in the year in question. All of this has then to be compared with the economy's total value. If that value is expanding rapidly enough, an apparent increase in government debt may still be consistent with that debt declining relative to the now higher-value economy, suggesting very crudely that taxes don't have to rise quite so quickly.

An economy's value, however, is determined both by the volume of activity (transactions) and the level of prices. In terms of the quantity theory (last seen in chapter 2), value is represented by PT. The more the price level, P, rises for any given volume of activity, the larger is the *value* of economic activity for any given *volume* of activity. Put another way, the higher an economy's inflation rate, the more sustainable is government debt, other things being equal.

As with so many other theoretical economic relationships, however, the 'other things being equal' condition is doing an awful lot of work. The big problem with the idea that a government can inflate away its debt is that interest rates may rise in response.[4] Specifically, if investors fear that a government is about to embark on an inflationary spree, they will demand compensation. If they don't get it, they may then shun the opportunity to lend to the government. The result is likely to be even higher interest rates and, as foreign lenders head for the hills, a weaker exchange rate. The government is then faced with a choice: either to tighten fiscal policy via higher taxes or public spending cuts (which may be politically unacceptable, at least in the short term), or else create even more inflation than creditors were anticipating in a bid to 'inflate away' government debt (a process that is only likely to be magnified as import prices rise in response to the weaker exchange rate and as wage earners rush to empty their cash balances).

Brazil's failed experiment

To be fair, it's possible to imagine a world in which companies and workers, governments and households, borrowers and lenders all anticipate a relatively high inflation rate, which in turn becomes a new 'steady state'. Arguably, Brazil tried to conjure up such a world in the decades following the end of the Second World War, attempting to live with an inflation rate far higher than anything that would be regarded as even remotely acceptable in today's developed world. Between 1950 and

1970, for example, wholesale prices in Brazil rose at an annual rate of 30 per cent, representing a sustained period of monetary destruction. Yet at the same time, national income in real terms expanded at an annual rate of 6.4 per cent.

On a superficial level, the decades after the Second World War were, in monetary terms, chaotic for Brazil. The first *cruzeiro*, introduced in 1942, lost value so quickly that it was replaced in 1967 by what was initially known as the *cruzeiro novo*. One *cruzeiro novo* was worth 1,000 of the old *cruzeiros*. Yet somehow the economy blossomed. That, at least, is what the headline figures suggested.

Underneath all this were myriad distortions. Very high rates of inflation were associated with increasingly negative real interest rates. In effect, Brazilian companies were being paid to undertake investments that were likely to be neither productive nor particularly profitable. The volume of capital spending may have been high, but the future returns on such spending were only likely to disappoint: the hurdle rate for investment was simply too low. Meanwhile, through a series of indexation measures known as 'monetary correction', inflation became institutionalised: and those who had the biggest political clout typically enjoyed the greatest inflation 'compensation', one reason why income inequality became a growing problem.

In the 1970s, it appeared that the Brazilian miracle was still on track. Although the exchange rate was vulnerable to frequent downward lurches – there were eleven devaluations against the US dollar in 1974 alone – economic growth held up remarkably well, particularly given the oil-related upheavals happening elsewhere. Indeed, the average annual increase in national income in the 1970s stood at 8.2 per cent, an improvement on what had gone before. Inflation had accelerated further – wholesale prices rose at an annual rate of around 37 per cent

– but frankly, who cared? Brazil was apparently an economy that had turned conventional economic thinking on its head.

Yet Brazil's luck – and it really was luck – was running out. Conventional economics bit back with a vengeance. From the mid-1970s onwards, petrodollars – the revenues built up by the world's oil producers in the aftermath of the 1973 oil price hike – found their way to Latin America via the US banking system. This recycling of oil revenues resulted in easy access to remarkably cheap credit, at least by the standards of the day. Brazil's external debt surged. Yet such generosity on behalf of Brazil's creditors proved to be no more than temporary. By 1980, Brazil's balance of payments current account deficit was approaching 9 per cent of national income. Unfortunately, with US interest rates now rapidly rising as Paul Volcker's Federal Reserve attempted to tame inflation at home, Brazil's ability to attract the necessary external funding dwindled rapidly. In other words, the balance of payments deficit had to shrink – and quickly.

That meant a rapidly falling exchange rate. Unfortunately, owing to the earlier epidemic of wage and price indexation, a weaker exchange rate – and thus higher import prices – simply prompted a rapid acceleration in domestic inflation. The hoped-for improvement in competitiveness vanished in an orgy of domestic wage and price increases. Annual inflation rose to around 100 per cent at the beginning of the 1980s, before accelerating even further. For the decade as a whole, annual inflation averaged a whopping 300 per cent. Inevitably, the second *cruzeiro* was replaced with the *cruzado*, itself replaced with the *cruzado novo* in 1989. Even then, the rot didn't stop. Through the next decade, Brazilian inflation averaged an annual 200 per cent. Per capita incomes, meanwhile, hardly budged. No longer was it possible to claim that higher inflation was a price worth paying for rapidly rising living standards.

Brazil is, admittedly, an extreme example of inflationary excess. Yet there are lessons to be learnt. First, although it might be possible to live with high inflation for years – even decades – inflation can nevertheless lead to a hugely unequal society. In Brazil's case, only those with political influence, for example, were able to enjoy the full protection of indexation. Put very simply, the rich got richer, while the poor were left behind. Success ultimately was a privilege enjoyed by an already privileged few. Second, it is easier to live with high inflation if your foreign neighbours are willing to indulge you: such indulgence, however, can disappear remarkably quickly in the light of a changing global macroeconomic environment, as occurred at the beginning of the 1980s. Third, opting for higher inflation is ultimately a political choice. For those countries with weak fiscal positions, reflected in poor tax revenue-collecting abilities or excessive public spending largesse, associated with the need to buy votes, resorting to inflation can be a tempting – if myopic – option. If uncorrected, however, myopia can lead to nasty accidents.

Central bank independence . . . or Richard Burton and Elizabeth Taylor?

The creation of independent central banks was intended to sever any connection between monetary and fiscal policy, at least as far as policymaking decisions were concerned. The idea was for central banks to bolster their inflation-fighting credentials, freed from the tyranny of the electoral cycle. More and more central banks followed the example set by Germany's independent Bundesbank back in the 1970s and 1980s. There was, however, one big difference. Germans knew their hyper-inflationary history and were content to have a monetary power-house that, at times, was willing to squash – via higher interest rates – a democratically elected government's excessive fiscal expansion. Other central banks did not enjoy such uniform support. As a result, the alleged separation between monetary church and fiscal state was – and is – mostly a fiction. History offers countless examples in which fiscal expediency trumps monetary stability. The two big macroeconomic levers are the economic equivalent of Elizabeth Taylor and Richard Burton, the Hollywood stars who were married twice and who were, perhaps, still in love when Burton died in 1984: occasionally separated but always destined to reconnect.[5]

In the first two decades of the twenty-first century, three versions of such 'coming together' have occurred: quantitative easing, the European Central Bank's sovereign debt programmes and – conceptually if not yet in reality – the ideas behind Modern Monetary Theory. Each 'coming together' has created – or threatens to create – heightened inflationary risk.

Quantitative easing: blurring the lines between monetary and fiscal policy

Quantitative easing emerged during the Global Financial Crisis. At the time, different central banks used different terms for what amounted to an attempt to provide monetary stimulus without having to cut official short-term interest rates. The Federal Reserve, for example, referred to its 'asset purchase program', largely because a relatively wide range of assets ended up on the Fed's balance sheet. In contrast, the Bank of England, for the most part, stuck to purchases of gilts – government bonds (or IOUs) – and it is the Bank of England terminology that has ultimately stuck.

One reason for the adoption of quantitative easing was simply that central banks were running out of conventional monetary bullets. Short-term interest rates were heading rapidly towards zero and, because cash offered a guaranteed zero nominal interest rate, there was an understandable fear that central banks would be perceived as impotent. As such, people might begin to hoard cash, anticipating the onset of another Great Depression. Their hoarding, in turn, would trigger a collapse in demand, the onset of deflation, an increase in bankruptcies and a surge in unemployment – in other words, precisely what they most feared. In that sense, President Roosevelt hit the nail on the head in his inaugural presidential address in 1933, in the midst of the Great Depression, when he asserted 'my firm belief that the only thing we have to fear is . . . fear itself'.[6]

Another reason behind the adoption of quantitative easing was a suspicion that the so-called 'transmission mechanism' between policy rates and the broader economy was broken. Multiple bank failures suggested that remaining banks were in no position to lend generously, even if lower interest rates were encouraging an increase in the number of would-be borrowers. It was as if the economic plumbing had stopped working: central banks were able to adjust the interest-rate thermostats on the walls of their economies, but the commercial banking boilers no longer had the power of old. Quantitative easing was designed to 'replumb' an economy. By buying government debt across a range of maturities, and thus driving borrowing costs across that range of maturities lower, pension funds and insurance companies would no longer be able to meet their future expected liabilities by 'playing it safe' through now very low-yielding government bonds. Instead, they would have to find higher returns for their policyholders by investing in riskier assets.

The intention was to drive risky asset prices higher, in the hope that companies would then be able to raise funds more easily via the capital markets.[7] Why worry about the inability of banks to lend, if another source of funding could be enhanced? To a degree, the approach worked: equity prices surged, as did corporate bond prices. Yet there was little in the way of any acceleration in capital spending and, for the most part, economic growth remained anaemic. The plumbing may have been rerouted, but there was little evidence that economies were really warming up.

What started off as an emergency measure designed to offer only temporary monetary succour evolved into a semi-permanent feature of the policymaking landscape. Fears of deflation refused to go away, partly because economies were unable to return to the growth rates of old. Yet with unemployment steadily falling, it appeared that the economic problem confronting policymakers stemmed less from an absence of demand and more from a shortage of supply. In other words, productivity growth was lamentably weak.

For the most part, monetary stimulus does little, if anything, to boost productivity. Indeed, as Brazil found in the 1950s and 1960s, it can actually make things worse, encouraging too much in the way of wasteful, non-productive, private-sector investment. Quantitative easing, however, does something else. By buying up government debt and placing it on the central bank's balance sheet, quantitative easing is a mechanism which removes the discipline that governments once faced from the so-called bond market vigilantes. These hungry investors spent their time prowling the financial savannah in search of fiscal or monetary weakness. When they found it, they pounced. The relevant bond market would come under heavy selling pressure, a government's borrowing costs would surge, and pressure would build to reverse what the vigilantes regarded – admittedly, not always fairly – as foolish policies.[8]

Quantitative easing is, in effect, a mechanism that keeps the vigilantes quiet, or at least encourages them to look for opportunities elsewhere. As a result, the discipline of old has been lost. Policymakers can choose to pretend that their policies are on track by pointing towards well-behaved bond markets. Yet the bond markets' good behaviour is a phantom; massive central bank bond buying is, after all, a form of asset market nationalisation, specifically designed to move prices away from where they would be in free-market conditions.

One consequence of this is that bond markets can no longer operate fully as 'early-warning systems' regarding potential policy error. The absence of such systems, in turn, means that inflationary fears appear on the radar screen far too late, creating a backward-looking complacency regarding inflationary risk. Indeed, even as inflation surged through 2021 and 2022, bond yields initially rose only modestly relative to history, in part reflecting a belief within financial markets – interestingly, not always shared among households and businesses – that short-lived inflation would be followed by recession, requiring more in the way of addictive quantitative easing.[9] That position, however, didn't allow for the possibility that, for any given level of economic activity, inflation was in danger of being significantly higher than it had been in the past. Investors, it seemed, were in danger of making the same mistakes their forebears had made in the 1960s and 1970s.

In some cases, quantitative easing has, unfortunately, increased what might best be described as the political risk associated with the use of supposedly independent monetary policies. Put simply, the fiscal fallout stemming from concerted monetary tightening is higher than it once was, thanks to a convoluted connection between monetary policy and fiscal sustainability.

The UK offers perhaps the most obvious example of this growing problem. The accountancy of quantitative easing is relatively straightforward.[10] In the UK's case, the purchase of gilts is carried out via the Bank of England's Asset Purchase Facility, financed through the creation of additional central bank reserves – in effect, deposits held at the Bank of England by commercial banks. For the public sector as a whole – government plus Bank of England – liabilities in the form of gilts have thus been replaced by liabilities in the form of central bank reserves. That sounds innocuous enough, but there is, nevertheless, an important implication for the public finances. In 2022, gilts had an average maturity of around thirteen years. Central bank reserves, however, are overnight money. If overnight policy rates – as set by the Bank of England – are unusually low, the public sector as a whole saves money: interest payments on bank reserves will be lower than interest payments on gilts would have been in the absence of quantitative easing. In other words, periods of loose monetary policy provide a windfall fiscal gain. Equally, however, periods of tight monetary policy – when policy rates are high and thus interest payments on bank reserves are larger than interest payments on gilts would have been in the absence of quantitative easing – provide a windfall fiscal loss. In effect, the overall shortening of the maturity structure of public debt – an inevitable consequence of quantitative easing – increases the fiscal sensitivity of monetary policy decisions. Periods of low short-term interest rates help improve fiscal stability, whereas periods of high short-term interest rates do exactly the opposite, particularly when government debt is very high relative to previous history.[11] Quantitative easing proves that, when it comes to monetary and fiscal relationships, Elizabeth Taylor and Richard Burton's voices can be heard from beyond the grave.

The 'other things equal' clause applies in this case, too. A strong productivity-led economic recovery associated with both higher interest rates and bountiful tax revenues would not be so worrying from a fiscal sustainability perspective. Indeed, the much-vaunted 'build back better' post-pandemic ambition – pushed by a diversity of politicians from left and right, including Joe Biden, Boris Johnson, Jacinda Ardern and Justin Trudeau – was consistent with a higher-growth, higher-revenue and higher-interest-rate economic outcome. In hindsight, however, no economy of note managed significantly to 'build back better'. True, the value of economic activity in most cases rose rapidly. That, however, was a result of too much inflation, even as the volume of national income remained depressed. Excessive inflation, in turn, may have resulted in part from timid central banks fearing they would be blamed by fiscally nervous governments for raising policy rates too quickly, in the process undermining the fiscal arithmetic. After all, the mantra was to 'build back better', not 'starve the government of money'.

For a few sovereigns more: the eurozone's fiscal challenge

The economic and financial issues that confronted the US in the aftermath of its Civil War have returned – with the volume turned down a few notches, perhaps – within the eurozone. Problems initially surfaced visibly with the eurozone sovereign debt crisis that followed the Global Financial Crisis. In truth, it was less a sovereign crisis and more a balance of payments crisis: northern European lenders – the equivalent of the victors in the American Civil War – were increasingly worried about what was happening to the funds they had poured into the eurozone periphery – the equivalent of the former Confederate states. A series of 'sudden stops' triggered economic collapse, most obviously in Greece, which suffered from what appeared to be an apocalyptic economic and financial meltdown.

The most visible sign of the crisis was, at least financially, the widening of government bond spreads: Portuguese, Italian, Irish, Spanish and, particularly, Greek government borrowing costs rose relative to those in, for example, Germany and the Netherlands. Although, superficially, it appeared that markets were pricing in a heightened risk of default, the truth was a little more subtle. Investors became fearful about the euro-zone's survival. In the absence of a system of regional fiscal transfers – of a type taken for granted within sovereign states, but which typically barely exist between sovereign states – the fear was that fiscal strains would ultimately blow the euro apart, with countries reluctantly forced to reintroduce their former national currencies. Under these circumstances, bond markets became proxy currency markets: an investor fearing the reintroduction of a rapidly depreciating Italian lira tomorrow, for example, needed extra compensation for holding Italian government bonds today. Yet higher Italian interest rates threatened to condemn Italy to persistent poverty.

At this point, Mario Draghi, the then-president of the European Central Bank, issued his 'magic words', promising to do 'whatever it takes' to ensure the future of the single currency and all those who sailed in it.[12] Thereafter, the European Central Bank – ostensibly the inflation fighter *par excellence* – became the effective guarantor of the euro's survival. In effect, it would buy the bonds of governments otherwise financially marooned, in a bid to prevent the system's collapse. The ECB thus found itself with three – potentially competing – roles: preserver of price stability, lender of last resort and now bond market bailer-out-in-chief.

When inflation was below target and threatening to dip into outright deflation, there was no real conflict: the promise of continued monetary stimulus and outright bond buying suited both the ECB's monetary aims and its desire to keep the eurozone whole. All that began to change in late 2021. As inflation rose, so nervousness about sovereign strains re-emerged. Through much of that year, Italian ten-year government bond yields over their German equivalents had hovered at around 1.25 per cent. By year-end, spreads had widened to 1.5 per cent. Seven months later, spreads had risen momentarily beyond 2.5 per cent. Admittedly, spreads weren't as wide as those that existed between Germany and non-eurozone countries – the US, Canada and Australia, for example – but that, frankly, misses the point. Outside the eurozone, there is currency risk. Within the eurozone, there isn't supposed to be any.

The ECB's response to this renewed market mayhem was to introduce a 'Transmission Protection Instrument' (TPI).[13] The idea was to 'support the effective transmission of monetary policy', in order to ensure 'that the monetary policy stance is transmitted smoothly across all euro area countries'. More specifically, the TPI

> can be activated to counter unwarranted, disorderly market dynamics that pose a serious threat to the transmission of monetary policy across the euro area ... the Eurosystem will be able to make secondary market purchases of securities issued in jurisdictions experiencing a deterioration in financing conditions not warranted by country-specific fundamentals.[14]

While the ECB's decision is understandable, it's difficult to see its intervention as anything other than another attempt to 'nationalise' parts of the bond market. What counts as 'unwarranted' or 'disorderly'? Can a committee based in Frankfurt really opine not just on the appropriate level for policy rates, but also on government borrowing costs for each individual country in the eurozone? We're back to the idea of the central bank as all-powerful, able to assess imbalances in ways that those mere mortals operating in financial markets are apparently ill-equipped to do.

The creation of the TPI was a response not so much to disorderly markets, but rather to the observed widening of bond spreads in response to mounting inflationary fears. An alternative way to consider the problem is to think about what kind of inflation rate might be acceptable in differing eurozone economies. Take, for example, Germany and Italy, both of which found themselves in the firing line of Vladimir Putin's gas pipeline politics in 2022. By September, German inflation was both higher than Italian inflation and in double digits – a remarkable reversal of fortune from the 1970s, when oil shocks had little lasting impact on German inflation, even as Italian inflation headed into the stratosphere.

Is this relevant? Potentially, yes. A properly functioning monetary union would include a political agreement allowing transfers of tax revenues from more privileged regions to their less privileged counterparts. It's what takes place, after all, between Massachusetts and Mississippi and between Milan and Monopoli. Importantly, the process is typically automatic – a consequence of having a federal (or nationwide) tax, benefit and spending system. The eurozone has only the bare bones of such a system, and so each funding 'emergency' requires a new monetary 'fix', particularly given the absence of a eurozone-wide finance ministry.

Now think of inflation as an alternative to a nationwide (or indeed euro-wide) fiscal system. Apply the lessons from the aftermath of the American Civil War. Back then, the creditors from the Northern states had no interest in allowing inflation to take root, recognising that doing so would shift the balance of economic adjustment: the higher the inflation rate, the bigger the rewards for Southern debtors and the bigger the risks for Northern creditors. Eurozone inflation has roughly the same effect. German and Dutch creditors would see their savings – at least in the form of cash and bonds – dwindle, while southern debts would, over time, be 'forgiven'. Admittedly, such a process would not be consistent with lasting price stability. If, however, the cost of raising interest rates high enough to bring inflation to heel was impending eurozone collapse, it's easy to see how the ECB might choose to accept higher inflation for a little while longer: it would be, in these circumstances, the mechanism behind a surrogate fiscal transfer. Whether it likes it or not, the ECB has been dragged into the fiscal realm because inflation is, *in extremis*, a fiscal tool. We are back to Taylor and Burton.

Modern Monetary Theory: as if history hadn't happened

With inflation seemingly dead and buried, it was perhaps not surprising that new economic ideas would emerge. After all, the achievement of low inflation had not proved to be an economic cure-all. Unemployment in some countries was still elevated, regional imbalances were sizeable, income inequality was high within countries (even if it had narrowed between countries), and a combination of technological advance and outsourcing meant that some workers – at least in Europe and North America – seemed trapped in dead-end jobs.

According to its proponents, Modern Monetary Theory (MMT) offered a partial solution. Its starting point is the idea that governments with access to a printing press, unlike households and companies (and members of the eurozone), cannot run out of money. They are currency 'issuers', not currency 'users'. As such, budget deficits are, from a solvency perspective, an irrelevance. Government debt, meanwhile, cannot be a constraint, because those governments with access to a printing press need never default. Inflation, meanwhile, 'is not caused by increases in monetary aggregates *per se*',[15] the Federal Reserve 'uses unemployed people as its primary weapon against inflation',[16] and monetary policy has only limited potency – at least regarding stimulus – because 'it works mainly by driving consumers and business into debt'.[17] Fiscal policy is far more effective, because, unlike 'currency-using' households and businesses, governments can always cover their debts by printing money: they are currency 'issuers'.

MMT turns the conventional macroeconomic thinking seen since the 1990s on its head. Fiscal policy, not monetary policy, should be used to regulate the economy. Macroeconomic management should be given to elected officials, not to technocratic central bankers. Unemployment should not be used as a mechanism to control inflationary pressures. Central banks should not be in the business of generating recoveries by encouraging excessive household or corporate leverage. Governments should create as many jobs as possible, using the printing press if necessary. The control of inflation – via fiscal, not monetary policy – should be the responsibility of governments alone. And, thanks to pressure from the ballot box, governments of whatever political hue will take that responsibility seriously. Apparently, it is only those who don't have to face democratic re-election – most obviously, those in the central banking fraternity – who are likely to mismanage the economy to the extent either that inflation runs out of control, or its defeat leads inevitably to recession.

As with conventional macroeconomic thinking, MMTers believe their approach will keep inflation under wraps. Yet it may be more plausible to argue that MMT has gained advocates only because inflation had been under wraps for so long. Suggesting, for example, that governments can be trusted to keep inflation under control is, frankly, at variance with the historical evidence. More than any other institution, governments are likely to enthuse about inflation, both because they control the printing press and because the alternatives to inflation – higher taxes, austerity, default – are too often politically unacceptable.

MMTers would argue that, with a printing press, there is no need to raise taxes to fund public spending. For them, taxes only serve other purposes. Macroeconomic regulation is one. And, for the more imaginative of their ilk, taxes apparently encourage people to go to work: 'tax liabilities create sellers of goods and services desiring government currency in exchange'.[18] Yet their description of the world misses out so much of what, through history, has linked government control of the printing press to inflation. Much of this historical reality has already made an appearance in this book.

Ultimately, governments are tempted to print money as an alternative, underhand, way of forcing populations to pay more taxes. The mechanism varies, depending on the circumstances; but the result, typically, is the same. Other things being equal, a big increase in government borrowing, funded by monetary expansion that in turn leads to higher inflation, will: (i) rob savers, by depressing real interest rates (the equivalent of a tax on wealth held in the form of cash); (ii) rob consumers, by forcing the exchange rate lower and by raising import prices (the equivalent of an increase in VAT on imported goods) or by forcing prices higher relative to wages (as happens during *what are inflation-protected assets?*

wartime, when scarce resources have to be diverted to military imperatives);[19] and (iii) rob the poor, whose meagre savings are more likely to be in cash than in inflation-protected assets and who are less likely to be able to negotiate effective protection against rising inflationary pressures. Others, including those with mortgages, those with pricing power (large companies, unionised workers) and, of course, those responsible for looking after a government's finances, may do well. The process is, however, both stealthy and profoundly undemocratic.

Worse, when inflation does make an appearance, MMTers tend to argue that the solution lies not in containing inflation in general, but instead either in limiting demand in the more problematic areas (most obviously energy) or in boosting supply. They base their views on an interesting interpretation of history. For example, in the 1980s, 'what ultimately brought inflation down was the negotiated peace treaty in the Mid-East[20] and the development of alternative sources of energy, namely natural gas, which benefited from deregulation under President Carter'.[21]

The recommendation in mid-2022 was to do something similar.

> [W]e need a negotiated resolution to the war in Ukraine. We also need to make (long-overdue) investments in renewable energy ... The Federal Reserve cannot bring down inflation because it cannot bring down the price of energy ... President Biden should level with the American people ... Ask people to ... avoid unnecessary travel ... [U]rge employers to ... accommodate work from home ... [M]ake public transportation ... free to all riders ... Ease backlogs at the ports ... Build housing![22]

All admirable stuff, perhaps, but by the time those words were written, a health pandemic had been followed by an inflation pandemic. Energy prices alone were not driving US inflation higher. Durable goods, non-durables, services and – belatedly – workers were all becoming more expensive. Waiting for a peace treaty to materialise, or hoping that supply would simply rise to meet demand, were acts of wishful thinking, not viable policy options in dealing with inflation. In 1940, John Maynard Keynes wrote his famous pamphlet *How to Pay for the War: A Radical Plan for the Chancellor of the Exchequer* because he rightly recognised that war was inflationary. His answer was complex, including a savings policy to secure 'deferred consumption' at war's end; but his recommendations did not begin with 'we need a negotiated resolution' with Adolf Hitler.[23]

It's tempting to conclude that proponents of MMT simply don't take inflation seriously. Like everyone else, they'd rather it wasn't there; but when it does materialise, they are quick either to explain it away or to offer unconvincing solutions, in a bid to avoid near-term economic pain. After all, it's a school of thought that believes the printing press – the most obvious threat to price stability in the modern era – is the easiest and most reliable way to fund government debt. They, too, adopt the Taylor and Burton approach, pretending that fiscal policies are entirely independent of their monetary equivalents.

But there is one big difference between the two approaches. Conventional frameworks abhor fiscal dominance over monetary policy: advocates fear that political expediency will only lead to heightened price instability; they also pretend, falsely, that the two policy levers can be kept separate – it's neater that way. By contrast, MMTers embrace fiscal dominance, based seemingly on a distorted version of history, in which governments somehow manage to avoid the temptations of the printing press. In their world, only the monetary authorities are not to be trusted. It's a world of fiction, not of carefully observed fact.

Governments and inflation: conclusions

Not all governments will go down the inflationary path. But the circumstances they face will help determine whether they do eventually succumb to temptation.

The frequency with which they do so depends partly on specific national histories. Brazil has found inflation to be a more acceptable outcome than, say, post-war Germany. Inflation is a mechanism to tax citizens in a stealthy, underhand fashion, typically deployed when other revenue-raising options – higher taxes, for example – are politically undesirable.[24] Structurally, some tax systems are simply more effective than others – one reason why some emerging markets find themselves resorting to inflation more often as a fiscal option than their developed market cousins.

Wartime provides the ultimate proof of inflation's useful role as a hidden tax. Whether the conflict is within a nation (as with the American Civil War) or between nations, the increase in military spending and the corresponding reduction in civilian spending can readily be achieved by printing money, thereby encouraging inflation to rise.

Following the Great Moderation, it's been all too easy to forget the role governments can play in the creation of inflation. Yet faith in both the independence of central banks and the effectiveness of inflation-targeting regimes has been accompanied by a hidden 'infiltration' of inflation-friendly institutional reforms, including quantitative easing and, within the eurozone, an increased 'stabilisation' role for the European Central Bank.

This infiltration is not directly an issue about the simple expansion of money supply, as many monetarists would tend to argue. Instead, it's a story about signal failures in bond markets, conflicts between monetary and fiscal stability, and – in the eurozone – a determination to prevent the crumbling of the single currency at any cost. Each of these themes threatens to allow inflationary pressures to come in through the back door. No one intended inflation to rise, perhaps, but the changing policy arrangements since the Global Financial Crisis have nevertheless made inflationary errors more likely.

Those that advocate shifting responsibility for the control of inflation to elected governments may believe that democratically elected politicians are better able than technocrats to achieve the right balance between, say, inflation and unemployment; but the historical evidence is absolutely not on their side. Left to their own devices, governments cannot help but be tempted by inflation. Central banks are there to discourage governments from responding to the siren voices. Giving government free rein would be the equivalent of untying Odysseus and emptying the beeswax from his crew's ears.[25] If Greek mythology is any guide, it wouldn't end well.

Having explained why governments succumb to inflationary temptation, it's now time to suggest why they would be best advised not to. Inflation, it turns out, is deeply, profoundly unfair.

yield x
tax charge (x)(tax)
net (1.0x) - (1.0x)(tax)

4

The Case for Resisting
Inflationary Temptations

*Weimar's King of Inflation – the 1970s focus on fairness – the
arbitrary creation of winners and losers – evading the taxman
– everyone wants a Ford Capri – the costs of monetary action –
demands for wage moderation in the modern era*

If the last chapter was ultimately a story about why governments can succumb to inflationary temptations, this chapter
provides what might be described as the compelling evidence
for the need to seek an antidote. Inflation can be very costly
indeed. Sometimes, however, its costs may be difficult to see
within the aggregate economic data.

The King of Inflation

Take, for example, the (admittedly extreme) case of Germany's
hyperinflation between 1918 and 1923. If the pre-1914 price
level averaged 100, the peak price level at the end of 1923 was

a remarkable 142,905,055,447,917. Stories surrounding this mass loss of monetary value are plentiful: the man who bought two bottles of beer at the same time, fearing that the second would cost him more if he waited until he'd consumed the contents of the first (a fine example of the idea that time is money); hitherto wealthy landlords made destitute because their – regulated – rental income didn't keep pace with rapidly rising repair costs; academics forced to sell their entire libraries in order to buy a loaf of bread.

The aggregate data, however, only serve to hide such individual traumas. German incomes per capita fell 7.8 per cent in real terms between 1918 – at the end of the First World War – and 1923 – the worst year of Germany's hyperinflation nightmare. Yet, over the same period, UK incomes per capita fell by a lot more. Admittedly, demobilisation had a huge impact on economic activity in the UK; but nevertheless, it suffered few of the financial deprivations that befell Germany. Why, then, did Germany's drop in living standards appear to be more modest than the UK's?

The answer is, in part, that Germany's hyperinflation created extreme losers and winners. Anyone with financial wealth was enormously vulnerable: inflation threatened to wipe out the value of any nominal paper assets. In contrast, those able to use leverage to purchase property – including factories – and to stockpile goods made a fortune. After all, they were able to borrow in marks that, in a handful of hours, would be hugely diminished in value.

Admittedly, any sensible would-be lender witnessing this monetary chaos would demand painfully high interest rates by way of compensation. The government, however, proved to be anything but sensible: its discount rate did rise – from an annual rate of 5 per cent at the beginning of 1922 to 12 per cent at the beginning of 1923, before reaching 90 per cent in September of that year. By that stage, however, the German inflation rate was vast: pick a number, add multiple zeroes, and you get a rough approximation.

Large companies able to gain access to loans at such absurdly low government-linked interest rates were, in effect, being paid handsomely to borrow: their 'debts' would disappear in a matter of days. They were like bears with access to limitless honeypots: they and their owners became very rich. For smaller companies, however, an interest rate of 30 per cent per day was more likely – an extreme version of the 'pay day' loans so controversial in the UK in the years following the Global Financial Crisis.

Chief among those who made their fortune in the midst of this monetary chaos was Hugo Dieter Stinnes (1870–1924), who, according to the 1922 edition of *Encyclopaedia Britannica*, was the grandson of one Matthias Stinnes, 'the founder of a firm in no great way of business at Mülheim in the Ruhr district'. Hugo, however, appeared to have more business acumen than his forebears, starting his own company dealing in coal while in his early twenties. He quickly branched out into the transportation business, purchasing a range of vessels designed to transport his coal by river and sea. Offices opened in Hamburg, Rotterdam and Newcastle. He became director of numerous industrial companies. By the outbreak of the First World War, he was already a multimillionaire.

This, however, was only the beginning. His fortune expanded hugely during the war, partly reflecting his ability to integrate businesses vertically, in a bid to achieve huge cost savings in support of a hoped-for German victory. Post-war – and like many other German businesspeople – he became increasingly nervous about a homegrown Bolshevik uprising. As such, he ended up funding the *Antibolschewistenfond*, and in 1920, he was elected to the Reichstag. Whether or not he provided funding for Adolf Hitler's fledgling National Socialists remains a matter of historical conjecture, although his sympathies appeared to be heading in that direction. What is not up for debate, however, is that during the hyperinflation, he became rich beyond his wildest dreams. Borrowing in Reichsmarks using hard foreign currency as collateral – he was, by this stage, a properly international businessman – Stinnes was, in effect, receiving a vast subsidy to further his business interests. In March 1923, his international reputation was secured with an appearance on the front cover of *Time* magazine, just after the French occupation of the Ruhr.[1] The accompanying article labelled Stinnes a 'coal magnate, multimillionaire, present "All-Highest" of Germany', and concluded that, 'like all mysterious figures who move in the no-man's land of international politics, he stands to win whichever side comes out on top'.[2] Elsewhere, he became known as the King of Inflation.

Stinnes's ascent was rapidly undone owing to an absence of antibiotics: he died following a routine gall bladder operation in 1924. Thereafter, his empire collapsed, even if traces of his business DNA live on in Deutsche Bahn (the railway company) and RWE (the German energy supplier). Yet his story provides an enduring lesson about inflation, even in the most extreme circumstances. Many people lose; some, however, win. Inflation can be a powerful, yet fundamentally undemocratic, means of redistribution. It may not destroy the aggregate economy, but it has the capacity to destroy many people within it.

Winners, losers and time travel

It's important to stress, however, that the impact of inflation in the creation of winners and losers is as much an *ex ante* threat as an *ex post* reality. Indeed, spells of high inflation can be periods in which *ex post* inequality of income or wealth ends up being relatively low. The path towards such an outcome, however, can be highly problematic.

One example is the UK's experience in the 1970s, when high and volatile inflation was, for the most part, associated with low levels of both income and wealth inequality (compared with what had gone before and what would happen later). For example, the share of wealth held by the richest 10 per cent of the UK population fell from almost 100 per cent in 1900 to 87 per cent in 1950, 78 per cent in 1960, 72 per cent in 1970 and 58 per cent in 1980. The share of income accruing to the richest 10 per cent, meanwhile, fell from 56 per cent in 1900 to 49 per cent in 1950, 39 per cent in 1960, 31 per cent in 1970 and 30 per cent in 1980.[3]

These numbers, however, may be misleading. First, they don't say anything about people's changing relative positions: it's possible, for example, for one family to become a lot richer from one year to the next, while another becomes a lot poorer, leaving the overall level of inequality unchanged – the aggregate masks the experience of the individual (for every Hugo Stinnes, there may be multiple examples of hitherto wealthy people forced into penury). Second, inflation is hardly the only influence on inequality: other factors include, *inter alia*, sex-equality legislation, globalisation, regional imbalances and, most obviously, the tax regime.

Another approach, therefore, is to attempt to travel back in time, to see how people perceived both the causes of, and the consequences stemming from, a shift from low to high inflation. Inevitably, the perceived causes varied, depending on the political narrative of the day. According to contemporary surveys, in both 1966 and 1975, 'greedy workers' – and, thanks to their unions, their collective wage claims – were the main

British scapegoats, most likely because these were the years in which the government of the day made its greatest effort to negotiate an incomes policy. For reasons that remain unclear, managers received less opprobrium, perhaps because their numerous (now well-documented) inefficiencies were not quite so visible. The 'world situation' was blamed by many, particularly following the rapid increase in commodity prices in general and, in late 1973, oil prices in particular. Other candidates included membership of what was then the European Economic Community (the UK joined this earlier manifestation of the European Union in 1973)[4] and, in a throwback to debates about the relative value of different coins, the impact of decimalisation. Intriguingly, the majority of those surveyed did not think the various governments of the day were to blame, presumably taking the rather fatalistic view that nothing could be done to deal with a problem that had come from nowhere, but which was proving to be remarkably irksome.[5]

The 'greedy workers' narrative was, counterintuitively, reinforced by the mid-1970s Labour government. Understandably, Harold Wilson and his colleagues wanted to tackle inflation, which by then appeared to be in danger of spiralling out of control; but they didn't want to do anything that might threaten higher unemployment – Labour was, after all, the party that stood for the workers, above all others. A voluntary 'social contract' was, apparently, just the ticket. The emphasis was on fairness, in part because people perceived inflation simply to be 'unfair', without necessarily knowing why.

The unfairness of being fair

A leaflet distributed in 1975 to households up and down the country entitled 'Attack on Inflation: A Policy for Survival' argued that persistently high inflation would 'greatly increase unemployment; threaten us with external bankruptcy; and gravely damage the social and economic fabric of the nation' (all under the heading 'JOBS: THE HEART OF THE MATTER' – even though, by then, inflation had very much become the heart of the matter). Yet, in his foreword, Prime Minister Wilson struck a less strident tone, meekly asking 'Are the government's measures fair?' and 'Will they work?' Noting the vote within Parliament in favour of adopting 'a pay increase limit of £6 a week', Wilson added that

> the debate in Parliament is over. Discussion continues in the country – in homes, on television and radio and in the newspapers, at trade union and party political conferences … the nation – all of us – must now decide how best to back the Government's programme. How we, as individuals and in organisations, can best help to beat inflation.[6]

It was hardly a ringing endorsement of the proposals made by a government that Wilson himself led. Indeed, although the focus on fairness and democratic decision making was understandable, it was already clear that the government knew the UK's inflation performance was far from ideal. The leaflet contained five 'facts', one of which stated that

> most other countries have succeeded in bringing down their rate of inflation. We have not yet succeeded … Britain's leading competitors in world markets now have the edge on us. Their prices are increasing at only half the rate of ours. And the gap is widening.

Given the danger, Wilson's disinflationary ambition was, to say the least, limited. He hoped to bring inflation down to 10 per cent by the end of 1975, and under 10 per cent by the end of 1976. The actual numbers turned out to be, respectively, 24.9 per cent and 15.1 per cent, way above the inflation rates in some of the UK's main trading partners.[7]

Attempts to be 'fair' backfired for an obvious reason: when living standards are under serious downward pressure (UK productivity growth in the 1970s was lamentably poor) and everyone is being asked to make a sacrifice, the temptation for the individual – or for that matter, company or union – not to cooperate is extremely high. The narrative is, after all, straightforward. Inflation is perceived to corrode people's incomes. That seems unfair. Thus it makes sense, where possible, to demand a wage increase by way of compensation. And those that can, will – particularly if the government itself is happy to promote fairness over, say, economic stability.

Efforts to control inflation, meanwhile, failed because the most popular solutions to the problem were ones that, ultimately, simply did not work. In the October 1974 British Election Study, respondents overwhelmingly rejected higher unemployment as a mechanism to bring inflation down. Austerity, in the form of spending cuts or higher taxes, was a little more acceptable, but understandably still not terribly popular. Across both Conservative and Labour voters, the one policy with tremendous support was strict wage controls. In effect, everyone would make a small sacrifice – evoking the Dunkirk spirit – for the common good.

Yet there were four big problems. First, as we've seen, inflation didn't fall quickly enough, suggesting that those making a small sacrifice were wasting their time: neither government nor electorate had a strong understanding of what, precisely, was causing inflation, so both parties naturally gravitated towards what appeared to be the least painful option. Second, the foreign exchange markets were totally unconvinced, with sterling dropping like a stone through 1975 and 1976, pushing import prices – and hence inflation – higher.[8] Third, with the 1976 IMF bailout, the UK ended up imposing a dose of painful – albeit necessary – monetary discipline, which contributed to a doubling of unemployment in the second half of the 1970s, compared with the first half. Fourth, wage restraint simply meant that the labour market couldn't function properly. Sometimes, it makes sense for companies to attract workers by boosting wages, in order to take advantage of potentially productive and profitable opportunities: strict wage controls prevented companies from doing so, thereby limiting the scope for successful economic expansion.

In hindsight, it's easy enough to suggest that, thanks to the IMF, monetarism finally arrived in the UK. Certainly Jim Callaghan – Wilson's replacement – and Denis Healey, his chancellor of the Exchequer, appeared to have conducted something of a *volte face*, introducing monetary targets to the UK for the first time. Moreover, even though the Callaghan government was weak, with Labour relying on the support of the Liberals to push legislation through between March 1977 and September 1978, there were signs later in 1978 that perhaps Callaghan could win a general election: through October and November, Labour moved ahead of the Tories in the opinion polls.

The Labour leadership, however, hadn't fully embraced monetarism: it was still intellectually and politically committed to the idea of wage restraint. But increasingly the workers were not. A 17 per cent pay settlement for Ford workers in late 1978 completely undermined the government's own 5 per cent guideline for public-sector employees. Multiple strikes then followed, in a late 1970s version of 'fear of missing out'. Road hauliers, gravediggers, refuse collectors, hospital staff: all were determined to smash through the government's wage 'ceiling'. During this 'winter of discontent', opinion polls decisively shifted: a narrow Labour lead disappeared, presaging a thumping Conservative victory the following May.

It's not difficult to see how the 'social contract' turned into something rather more antisocial. Wage controls were only likely to remain popular if they helped deliver significantly lower inflation. They did nothing of the sort, largely because inflation wasn't just a consequence of excessive wage settlements. With inflation remaining high, it was inevitable that eventually the social contract would break down. Policymakers, encouraged by survey results, had misdiagnosed the inflationary problem, a warning to any politician tempted to make policy based on focus groups. That misdiagnosis, in turn, meant that many workers began to regard the wage controls as utterly pointless, serving only to guarantee real pay cuts.

The supermarket analogy

Stopping inflation in these circumstances was incredibly difficult. Once one group of workers had achieved an inflation-busting pay increase, others wanted to follow suit. No one wanted to be left behind.

Consider a simple analogy. Imagine that shoppers are queuing at the supermarket checkouts, their trolleys laden with food. Every few minutes, a trolley's contents are processed, the bill is paid, the car is loaded, and a happy shopper goes home ready to replenish the kitchen cupboards. The store manager then arbitrarily decides to stop serving the remaining queuing customers. They are told to go home empty handed, their efforts to secure their weekly groceries utterly futile. They will understandably be angry. Indeed, they might resort to violence or some other form of protest. They have seen others leaving the shop with bags full of produce. They, however, will have no food on their plates that night, thwarted in their ambition by the capriciousness of a malevolent supermarket boss.

In the real world, shops have well-publicised opening and closing times, so that the doors are closed to new customers, even as existing customers are still queuing up to pay. It makes sense, commercially, to manage people's expectations. After all, customers don't like to be left disappointed.[9] In contrast, during periods of high inflation, wage negotiations turn into a free for all. Without any 'rules of the game', it's a case of 'dog eat dog'. In that kind of atmosphere, the first casualty is fairness. The failure of successive British governments in the 1970s reflected not just an inability to understand the causes of inflation, but also their focus on fairness – via incomes policies – when fair outcomes were increasingly difficult to deliver.

Worse, stopping inflation under these circumstances is incredibly difficult. No politician wants to be the supermarket manager, because, unlike supermarket managers, politicians generally want to retain their popularity with the electorate. They're typically not in the business of shutting the store before everyone has had a chance to do their shopping. As such, the shopping just continues – or, in the case of inflation, prices and wages continue to spiral upwards. At that point, fatalism threatens to take over. As two economists writing about the UK's excessive inflation rate in the mid-1970s lamented, 'it may be the case that this degree of [wage and price] flexibility varies from country to country, and where there are strong trades unions and a dominant oligopolistic industry, the problem is worse'.[10]

Wealth vulnerabilities: the Stinnes effect more generally

Being left behind in the midst of a wage price spiral isn't much fun. Equally, seeing one's wealth being destroyed by a sustained period of either rising or falling prices – a period in which money either loses or gains value – isn't a barrel of laughs either. One way to show the difference is through two contrasting periods of twentieth-century US history, comparing the real (inflation-adjusted) returns on a range of assets, from bank deposits through to long-term government bonds, the stock market and real estate.

As a decade, the 1930s were something of a rollercoaster, with both the Great Depression and a later smaller depression combining with a general trend towards deflation. For the decade as a whole, prices fell by a little over 12 per cent. Over the same period, real estate was the worst performer, with a real return of only 9.2 per cent – considerably worse than money on deposit, which returned a real 20.5 per cent. For all the extra risk reflected in their catastrophically bumpy ride, equities managed 24.2 per cent, only a tiny amount more. Lending long term to the government was by far the most rewarding enterprise, with a total real return of 69.8 per cent.[11]

Now compare those numbers with the 1970s, a decade in which prices rose 117 per cent. Nothing did well, partly because higher oil prices meant that, as an economy, the US was simply worse off than it had been previously. Yet the relative performance of the different asset classes shifted enormously. During the 1970s, the worst places to be in real terms were cash savings (down 11.2 per cent) and government bonds (down 35.1 per cent). It was possible to squeeze out positive real returns from equities (up 4.2 per cent) and real estate (up 5.5 per cent), but on the whole, it was a decade in which savers and wealth accumulators were heavily penalised in real terms, in part owing to the unexpected persistence of inflation. The oft-made claim that periods of inflation are best dealt with by investing in so-called 'real assets' – those that make a direct claim on some aspect of an economy's future – is true, but only in a relative sense. It says more about the disastrous impact of inflation on bonds and cash than it does about the absolute merits of the other alternatives.

In fact, the best strategy in the 1970s would have been to borrow heavily in the form of cash, and then invest the funds raised in equities, real estate or, even better, physical assets, adopting the path used by Hugo Dieter Stinnes in early-1920s Weimar. Debts would be eroded by inflation – as reflected in the negative real returns on bank deposits and government bonds – but there would have been some modest gain in the value of so-called real assets. The group best placed to take advantage were first-time buyers, whose mortgages would be eroded by both negative real interest rates and rapidly rising nominal incomes (unless, of course, they found themselves joining the growing ranks of the unemployed). The worst placed were those in rental accommodation, with limited savings in the form of cash (diversification is only to be recommended if a person can afford to take modest losses from time to time on a portfolio of risky assets), and those who lacked bargaining power in the workplace: poor pensioners, non-unionised workers, those on benefits of one kind or another, generally the most vulnerable in society.

Rich and poor savers: some are more vulnerable than others

In the UK, savings patterns at the end of the 1970s confirmed these conclusions. Around 39 per cent of the bottom quarter of income earners had interest-bearing savings; 35 per cent owned their homes; 68 per cent had life assurance; and only 4 per cent owned stocks and shares. The equivalent figures for the top quarter of the income distribution were, respectively, 67 per cent, 71 per cent, 83 per cent and 16 per cent.[12] Successive governments' attempts at delivering fairness were undermined not just by the failure of incomes policies to keep a lid on wage settlements, but also by the fact that little effort was made to consider people's starting positions regarding the nature of their wealth.

Many suffered. Some got lucky, at least initially. Then, however, the taxman came along. The top rate of income tax rose from 75 per cent in 1973/1974 to 83 per cent the following year. To make things worse for the gilded classes, an investment income surcharge of 15 per cent was added, implying that the highest earners in society were facing a marginal tax rate on some of their income of 98 per cent. Whether or not such rates of confiscation were fair was, frankly, beside the point. Those faced with such rates simply employed excellent accountants – or else went into voluntary exile. The list is long and, in many cases, famous: John Barry, the composer of numerous James Bond songs; Shirley Bassey, the singer of some of those songs; Guy Hamilton, the director of *Goldfinger*, *Diamonds are Forever* and *Live and Let Die*; Sean Connery (Bond number one); Roger Moore (Bond number three);[13] Marc Bolan, the man behind the band T. Rex; David Bowie; Michael Caine; Rod Stewart; and – for one year and one year only – every member of Pink Floyd.[14]

It is easy enough to argue that this motley bunch of Hollywood stars, Bond heroes and rock gods selfishly went offshore to avoid paying their taxes when the UK was in desperate economic trouble. Yet even if that were true, it is surely not the most relevant conclusion. For those governments devoted to fairness, a failure to recognise that inflation itself is horribly unfair is likely to end in disaster. Allowing inflation to fester simply increases accusations of unfairness, which, in turn, leads to draconian tax policies, with all their unintended consequences – one of which is the creation of a huge tax avoidance industry.

Everyone wanted a Ford Capri

Policymakers knew, of course, that inflation was unfair. In a section of the aforementioned 'Attack on Inflation' headed 'Rough Justice', Harold Wilson's scriptwriters noted that the anti-inflation programme

> *is* rough, because the crisis called for tough measures. But it is fair ... because everybody, except the lower-paid, is called on to accept some cuts in living standards until the programme begins to bite on prices ... because the £6 pay limit means that the lower-paid can get proportionately most, and ... because there are provisions to help the worse-off ... Pensioners and people on social security will get further increases ... Other measures are designed to help housewives ... [emphasis in original]

Yet the truth was that no amount of voluntary pay restraint was likely to work, for the simple reason that wage pressures were, in effect, an endogenous part of a broader inflationary process. Policymakers may have recognised this, but feared that acting to halt inflation in its tracks by, for example, tightening monetary policy threatened to be, in the short term, both too painful and too provocative.[15] Far easier, then, to suggest that individuals and the groups they belonged to should exercise voluntary restraint. At the rear of the 'Attack' leaflet, a statement from the prime minister claimed: 'One man's pay rise is not only another man's price rise: it might also cost him his own job – or his neighbour's job.' Yet for many such men (in an unfortunate sign of the times, women seemingly appeared only as housewives), the statement could have been rephrased to say: 'One man's brand new Ford Capri is not only the source of his neighbour's envy: it might even encourage his neighbour to demand his own pay rise, so that he, too, can buy the car of the moment.'

Fearing action over inaction

One simple way of demonstrating UK policymakers' reluctance to get to grips with inflation in the 1970s is to compare average inflation rates with the average level of policy rates decade by decade. A word of warning beforehand, however. In the 1950s and 1960s, when the UK's primary monetary objective was the prevention of devaluation, and when exchange controls were used with considerable enthusiasm, the relationship between interest rates and inflation did not need to be terribly close: the focus of policy was, instead, on stabilising the balance of payments to prevent a run on the pound. Things changed in the early 1970s, when sterling floated on the foreign exchange rates: freed from an external monetary constraint, the UK ideally needed to impose a domestic monetary constraint. For much of the time, it chose not to.

Table 4.1 provides the results. In the 1960s, short-term interest rates were considerably higher than inflation, partly because the UK was engaged in an ultimately futile battle to prevent a sterling devaluation. In the event, sterling took the plunge in 1967. Four years later, with the collapse of the Bretton

Table 4.1: Fighting inflation: monetary policy matters

	Policy rates	Inflation	Real policy rates
1950s	4.1	4.4	-0.3
1960s	6.1	3.9	+2.2
1970s	10.1	12.8	-2.7
1980s	12.0	5.6	+6.4
1990s	7.8	2.7	+5.1
2000s	4.0	2.1	+1.9

Sources: Bank of England, author's calculations: ten-year arithmetic averages for policy rates, ten-year geometric averages for inflation rates

Woods system of fixed but adjustable exchange rates, sterling floated (although, given its rapid decline through much of the 1970s, it might be more accurate to say that sterling sank). The 1970s therefore provided a test: could policymakers replace an external 'discipline' (in the form of an exchange-rate constraint) with an internal discipline (in the form of, say, a money supply or inflation target)?

If actions speak louder than words, the answer was a resounding 'no'. Even though policy rates were a lot higher in the 1970s than in the 1960s, inflation was higher still. Those who could were being paid to borrow. Admittedly, the gap between the inflation rate and policy rates was tiny, compared with the gap that had opened up in hyperinflationary Weimar half a century earlier. But nevertheless, the principle was the same: for those with access to credit, it made sense to borrow more rather than less. To be fair, those who did so had to be confident that high inflation was likely to persist for a while – in other words, their expectations of inflation mattered as much as the current inflationary reality; but given the messages emanating from governments at the time, it wasn't a difficult conclusion to reach. In these circumstances, the chances were that nominal incomes (or PT, as first outlined in chapter 2) would expand rapidly. Given that, in real terms, the 1973 oil shock had made the country considerably worse off, it was equally likely that any expansion in PT would be driven by rapidly rising P, even as T fell. In other words, UK monetary arrangements in the 1970s almost guaranteed lasting stagflation.

The relationship between policy rates and inflation totally changed in the 1980s. Whether those who voted for Margaret Thatcher in 1979 quite got what they bargained for remains unclear, but nevertheless, in monetary terms, there was a decisive change in regime. Interest rates in the 1980s were even higher than they had been in the 1970s, yet inflation was a lot lower. The costs were, initially, enormous: soaring unemployment, mass deindustrialisation and widening regional inequality. Might those costs have been lower had inflation been tackled more aggressively ten years earlier? Perhaps. Certainly, the evidence from West Germany and other inflation-hating countries suggested as much: their earlier monetary actions led to both lower inflation and smaller increases in unemployment. Credibly establishing the monetary rules of the game, it turns out, is of the utmost importance.

Back to the 1970s

Allowing inflation to fester creates multiple 'supermarket' cases. Fear of being left behind turns into an epidemic. Mistrust builds and, alongside it, uncertainty rises. If a person's or business's relative position in the economic pecking order is no longer easily predictable, the chances are that decisions will be postponed, cancelled or made under false pretences (Brazil's wasteful investment, as outlined in chapter 3, is a case in point). The full impact of such distorted decision making may only emerge over years, if not decades. The likelihood is, however, that the arbitrary emergence of winners and losers is associated with a smaller economic pie than might otherwise have been the case. Debauching the currency may not always lead to revolution, but the economic costs can be very high. In the UK's case, the increase in living standards in the 1970s was below par: a gain of only 20 per cent, compared with 25 per cent in the 1960s and 27 per cent in the 1980s. The UK's 1970s experience was also worse than in other countries grappling with the same external shocks: over the same decade, German living standards rose 30 per cent, while those in France rose 29 per cent. Both had much lower inflation and better productivity growth. Intriguingly, the roles were reversed in the following decade, during which the UK – with a rapidly falling inflation rate – outsprinted both its near neighbours.[16]

The slow pace at which the costs of inflation tend to emerge is one reason why, all too often, it is allowed to fester. Stopping inflation in its tracks is immediately costly – in the form of higher interest rates and, possibly, recession. Allowing inflation to persist, however, is likely to lead to even higher costs longer term. Inflation ultimately undermines the fabric of society. Too often, however, those tasked with controlling inflation resort to exhortations regarding wage- and price-setting behaviour, as if somehow acts of verbal persuasion are likely to succeed. Andrew Bailey, governor of the Bank of England, channelled his own inner Harold Wilson in 2022, saying 'we do need to see a moderation of wage rises, now that's painful. But we do need to see that in order to get through this problem more quickly.' In response, Sharon Graham, general secretary of the Unite union, argued that 'workers didn't cause inflation or the energy crisis so why should they pay for it?'[17] In 2022, at least, it appeared that the language of the 1970s had returned.

The unfairness of inflation: conclusions

Once established, inflation is a deeply unfair process. Often the focus of such unfairness is the 'passive' impact of inflation on income and wealth: rising prices make people worse off and have a bigger impact on some forms of saving than on others. Yet it is the 'active' response to such perceived unfairness that can make matters a lot worse. Some in society are better able to protect themselves than others. In the former camp are the likes of Hugo Stinnes, large companies with pricing power and unionised workers with wage-setting power. In the latter are poor pensioners, those with limited cash savings and those on benefits. Those who 'win' are typically blamed by those who 'lose', a process that diverts attention from inflation's root causes.

Acting directly to protect people's incomes or wealth may, at times, be politically and morally necessary; but doing so typically deals only with symptoms, not with the root causes. Worse, the longer those root causes are ignored, the more expensive the process of 'bailing out' is likely to become. Particularly after an energy price shock – the quadrupling of oil prices at the end of 1973 or the tenfold increase in natural gas prices in 2021 and 2022 – bailouts serve only to draw a veil over a new, poorer economic reality.

Ignoring people's starting positions regarding wealth and savings means that many of the prospective inequities stemming from inflation go unheeded. Inflation is not just a story about the rising prices of goods purchased in shops: it is also a mechanism by which some people's claims on future production will rapidly diminish over time. Persistently rising prices ultimately destroy the value of money and, hence, cash savings.

Inflation's impact on society is not instantaneous. For all the – justifiable – headlines generated regarding food and energy prices, inflation is a slow-moving and stealthy adversary. One reason is simply that policymakers recognise that dealing with inflation is potentially painful. In the short run, therefore, it is easier to blame inflation on, say, external shocks, and then take credit for actions which, in themselves, do nothing to bring inflation to heel. The result, unfortunately, is inaction regarding the underlying drivers of inflation, increasing the chances of its persistence over the medium term.

Once inflation is established, and once its unfairness is recognised, there comes a time when it has to be dealt with. Some options, it turns out, are considerably better than others, largely because some simply do not work. The next chapter explains why.

5

How to Get Rid of Inflation . . . and How Not To

The Phillips curve – the Friedman/Phelps attack – the 'rational expectations' revolution – Sargent's hyperinflations – why modest inflations are more problematic – the failure of price and wage controls – the energy subsidy 'adding up' problem – expectations/rules of thumb – explaining Manchester United's fall from grace

To recap, inflation is a phenomenon that involves not just money, but also beliefs, social conventions and trust. Too often, governments are unable to resist the temptation to take the inflationary route, even if it might eventually end in tears. Monetary and fiscal arrangements can be kept separate from time to time, but they are always destined to re-establish what can too often prove to be a toxic Burton–Taylor relationship. That toxicity, in turn, can produce profound unfairness within society, in which the fear of being left behind threatens the political status quo.

Delaying the operation

Getting rid of inflation in these circumstances is, to say the least, difficult. While people won't want to suffer its toxic effects, they also fear the consequences of stopping it: and so, too, do their political leaders. Like a patient with a bunch of nasty symptoms, policymakers in a country suffering from inflation may choose to put off the operation ultimately required to deliver a cure: better, in the short term, for the patient to suffer the effects of inaction, than to have to endure the (possibly even more painful) post-operative rehabilitation, for which a nation's leaders will inevitably be blamed.

Until the post-pandemic acceleration in inflation, there was a sense within the central banking community that these difficulties belonged only in the pages of the dusty textbooks nestling on the shelves of academic libraries, and not in the here and now. The standard argument was simple: with the right institutions and the right policies, there was no reason for inflation to persist. Yes, there would be occasions when inflation would temporarily move away from target – the pre-Global Financial Crisis spike in oil prices provides a good example; but so long as policymakers were credible and transparent in their decision making, these temporary distortions would not evolve into something more sinister. Households, companies and financial market participants would understand that, faced with an inflation rate threatening to run out of control, a credible central bank will nudge policy rates higher, thus keeping a lid on any second-round wage–price spiral. Taken to its logical conclusion, the expectation of rate increases alone should be enough to temper inflationary fears, allowing a fully credible central bank to change official interest rates only rarely and by very small amounts.[1]

Curves and rationalities

The origins of this framework can be traced all the way back to the inflationary debates of the 1960s and 1970s. For much of that period, policymakers thought they had found the economic equivalent of the Holy Grail. The Phillips curve – beloved of so many economics textbooks – seemed to suggest that there was an exploitable trade-off between unemployment and inflation: you could have a little less of the former, in exchange for a little more of the latter (or vice versa).[2] Meanwhile, the Keynesian consensus held that fiscal policy was the only demand-management game in town (under the Bretton Woods system, monetary policy typically had the subservient role of helping stabilise the exchange rate, unless foreign exchange reserves were falling short, at which point interest-rate policy temporarily became dominant).[3]

There was, however, something rather obviously wrong with the Phillips curve, at least from a policy perspective. The idea seemed to be that people could be 'fooled' into accepting higher inflation – and, hence, lower 'real' pay – in exchange for a lower unemployment rate. If, however, inflation was permanently higher, it wouldn't take long for this new state of affairs to feed through into people's expectations. Workers would then begin to demand an 'expected inflation plus' wage increase. Repeated over a number of years, the implication was that any attempt to keep unemployment lower than its so-called 'natural' rate through macroeconomic policy stimulus would only lead to accelerating inflation, with no lasting reduction in unemployment. Seen this way, the long-run Phillips curve was vertical: the supposed 'trade-off' was a statistical illusion.

Milton Friedman[4] and Edmund Phelps,[5] who independently reached the same conclusion in the late 1960s, did so

not so much because they had come up with a way of meas-
uring people's expectations, but rather – embracing the *a priori*
spirit of David Ricardo during the Bullionist Controversy
described in chapter 2 – they regarded policymakers' claims
as foolish *ex ante*. Why would anyone ignore the possibility
that prospective inflation might be higher, and thus real
wages lower? Given half a chance, prices and wages would
both rise in such circumstances. This was a view that seemed
to capture the economic disasters of the 1970s better than
the conventional Keynesian alternatives, which mostly required
the use of incomes policies of one kind or another to keep a
lid on inflation, a process that was apparently driven by the
competing claims of different centres of power in society –
companies, unions – and not by inappropriate monetary
policies.

This, in turn, triggered the 'rational expectations' revolution
led by Robert Lucas and Thomas Sargent. They argued, in
effect, that if people behaved as Phelps and Friedman had
described, the world had to be seen in a 'forward-looking'
fashion: what happened today depended in part on what people
believed would happen tomorrow. And if everyone shared the
same view of how an economy operated, there were severe limits
as to what policymakers could hope to achieve: in particular, if
the public recognised that policymakers were about to embark
on a strategy that was unsustainable over time, it would immediately adjust its expectations, thus rendering the strategy unsustainable immediately. For macroeconomists, it was possible to
reach one of two conclusions. The first, nihilistic, possibility was
to accept that policy could achieve absolutely nothing of note,
leaving the economy on a so-called 'random walk'. The second,
optimistic, conclusion was that shifting away from poorly

thought-out policy decisions to well-understood policy rules could deliver significant benefits.

Sargent's Big Inflations

In 1982, Sargent went a stage further. Frustrated by gloomy prognostications about the perceived costs of eradicating well-established inflation, he used historical case studies to show that, with a credible and well-understood reform of institutional arrangements, it was possible to shift sustainably towards a lower inflation rate, at relatively low cost. In 'The Ends of Four Big Inflations',[6] Sargent threw down the gauntlet:

> an alternative 'rational expectations' view denies that there is any inherent momentum in the present process of inflation ... people expect high rates of inflation in the future precisely because the government's current and prospective monetary and fiscal policies warrant those expectations ... it is actually the long-term government policy of persistently running large deficits and creating money at high rates which imparts the momentum to the inflation rate.

Sargent's focus was on four big European inflations in the 1920s: the Weimar trauma described in chapter 4, alongside the inflationary experiences of Austria, Hungary and Poland. Among his key observations – based on a detailed quantitative assessment of each country's experience – were:

1. In all four cases, excessive inflation was linked to enormous and persistent budget deficits. We're back to the Burton–Taylor problem outlined in chapter 3.

2. The end of the inflationary periods came quickly, thanks to 'deliberate and drastic fiscal and monetary measures'.
3. In the light of these 'measures', prices immediately stabilised both domestically and on the foreign exchanges.

What were these 'magic' measures? The first was the creation of an independent central bank 'legally committed to refuse the government's demand for additional unsecured credit' (in other words, there was to be no deficit financing via the printing of money). The second was to place the government's finances on a sustainable course, so that any borrowing could ultimately be financed credibly via future tax revenues. In effect, Sargent recognised the Burton–Taylor problem, embraced the need for the relationship between fiscal and monetary policy to be credibly defined through a series of rules and prohibitions, and argued that, in this way, inflation could be defeated relatively painlessly.

Some like inflation . . .

The main problem with the argument, however, is that defeating hyperinflations may – counterintuitively – be easier than defeating modest inflations. Although some people – the likes of Hugo Stinnes, most obviously – may benefit, hyperinflations ultimately destroy societies. Normal economic life simply cannot take place. Any government offering a credible alternative, particularly when backed by the international community (either the leading superpower back in the day or, in modern times, institutions like the IMF), is likely to receive support from most of its citizens: few, after all, are likely to be enthusiasts for the preservation of a hyperinflationary status quo.[7] More moderate rates of inflation, however, suffer from the supermarket problem: too many people benefit from its presence and, in the process of stopping it, too many people fear they might lose out.

... but many don't like the costs of its removal

Sargent defended his historical examination by suggesting that 'the four incidents ... are akin to laboratory experiments in which the elemental forces that cause and can be used to stop inflation are easiest to spot'. He went on to argue that 'these incidents are full of lessons' for the 'less drastic' inflation the US was facing in the early 1980s.

To which the right response is 'Yes, but ...'. As it turned out, the removal of inflation in the early 1980s was more painful than might have been imagined, suggesting that 'rational expectations' weren't all they were cracked up to be. The main problem was the fear of U-turn, of policy reversal, of an absence of political credibility. The removal of inflation in the US was associated with not one, but two recessions in the early 1980s. Paul Volcker, the inflation-busting chair of the Federal Reserve, had to deal with an initially rebellious Federal Open Market Committee, the team responsible for setting US interest rates. Monetary tightening coincided not with the fiscal conservatism advocated by Sargent, but instead with the huge Reagan-era fiscal expansion, a combination that led to enormously high 'real' interest rates. Those, in turn, triggered a powerful and sustained rally in the value of the US dollar on the foreign exchanges, leaving other countries facing currency crises. Among the worst hit were Brazil and other Latin American economies which, as we have seen, succumbed to hyperinflation, currency collapse and, eventually, default. Indeed, a cynic might argue that American disinflationary policies worked not just through domestic channels, but importantly, via economic collapse elsewhere: other countries' weakness, after all, contributed to lower global prices and, hence, lower prices for goods and services imported into the US from elsewhere.

A similar set of – admittedly more localised – difficulties occurred in the UK. Following Margaret Thatcher's general election victory in May 1979, unemployment continued to soar. By the autumn of 1980, 2 million people were officially out of work, prompting some in her own party to demand a so-called policy U-turn. Her response at the October 1980 Conservative Party Conference subsequently became embedded in her party's folklore:

> To those waiting with bated breath for that favourite media catchphrase, the 'U-turn', I have only one thing to say: 'You turn if you want to. The lady's not for turning!'

Whether or not her words were directly prompted by the rational expectations revolution, they were certainly consistent with the revolution's message. It wasn't good enough simply to try a policy for a year or two and then abandon it. Instead, people had to be persuaded that the policy would be adhered to through thick and thin. Such acts of political persuasion, however, take time. And time, in turn, can use up huge amounts of political capital. Both violent insurrection and the ballot box end up getting in the way.

In the UK's case, an extra ingredient contributed to what proved to be a highly unequal distribution of the costs associated with the reduction in inflation. A combination of high interest rates and North Sea oil placed tremendous upward pressure on sterling.[8] The resulting collapse in manufacturing competitiveness led to vast amounts of regionally concentrated 'hollowing out': Londoners emerged relatively unscathed, even as vast swathes of Midlands industry were obliterated. Such inequalities of outcome meant that opposition to Thatcher's policies persisted for years to come. That persistence, in turn, meant that the adjustment costs were higher than Sargent and his ilk ever anticipated.

Still, as the 1980s gave way to the 1990s, the medicine, unpleasant though it was, appeared to be working. There were, admittedly, painful interruptions – most obviously what became known as the 'Lawson boom', during which inflation in the UK reaccelerated and interest rates soared. Little by little, however, inflation around the world became increasingly quiescent, interest rates tumbled in anticipation of continued price stability, and the political argument was won: more and more, the central banks became independent; inflation targeting (the 'end game' nominal framework after earlier experiments with money supply and exchange-rate targeting had been abandoned) became ubiquitous; and governments typically delivered what might best be described as cautious fiscal plans. Policies that had once been regarded as part of a right-wing, free-market cult had become part of the conventional wisdom. It wasn't difficult to see why: one of the worst economic bogeymen had apparently been slain.

Price and wage controls: a chequered history

At the same time, earlier 'inflation-busting' policies had apparently been consigned to the scrapheap of 'bad ideas in history'. Chief among them were price and wage controls. As Harold Wilson's government discovered in the 1970s, these don't always work very well. Time and again, however, they reappear. Governments do not like to be told they are directly responsible for an increase in inflationary pressures. There is a lack of understanding regarding the source of those inflationary pressures. And, most obviously, broad-brush inflation can be very unfair.

We first came across the inflationary excesses of successive Roman emperors in chapter 2. One of those rulers, Diocletian, was directly responsible for one of the first recorded instances of price controls.[9] The 'Edict on Maximum Prices' was issued in 301 CE and imposed maximum prices for at least 900 commodities (including for a male lion), as well as maximum rates for various kinds of freight and for around 130 different categories of labour. The inflationary excesses of the previous three centuries had developed, in part, because the empire found itself at near-continuous war on numerous fronts and had to discover a way of funding an ever-increasing wage bill for its soldiers. Debasing the coinage was the obvious answer. Diocletian and his advisers, however, concluded that persistent price increases had little to do with currency debasement, and a lot more to do with greedy speculators of one kind or another.

> We decree that if anyone, in his boldness, strive against the form of this statute, he shall undergo a capital penalty. And let not anyone suppose that a hardship is being enacted, since the observation of restraint is present and available as a safe haven for avoiding the penalty. To the same penalty also will be subject that person who from his eagerness to buy colludes with the greed of the seller contrary to the statute ... [and] the punishment ought to be even more serious for someone who initiates a scarcity [by hoarding].[10]

Even though most people would agree that capital punishment is a tougher sanction than, say, an increase in interest rates, the policy didn't work. Despite the threat of capital punishment (or a fate even worse than death, if the statute is to be believed), farmers understandably refused to part with their products, not keen to sell at below the perceived 'market price'. The resulting shortages triggered food riots. In some cases, the farmers were effectively forced into serfdom. Occupations subject to 'wage ceilings' not surprisingly became increasingly unpopular: the resulting labour shortage was dealt with by forcing children to follow their parents' occupations – the equivalent of creating a dynasty in Victorian times of, say, leech collectors or toshers.[11] Miserable jobs with no means of escape only added to the misery.

It was only with Constantine's ascent to power in 306 CE that the edict was repealed. With the introduction of the gold *solidus*, Constantine enacted the kind of currency reform that became a regular feature of Brazil's inflationary experience seventeen centuries later. Admittedly, a currency reform on its own provides no guarantee of price stability; but it is a natural next step when a policy of maximum prices (or price and wage ceilings) fails by interfering corrosively in the functioning of markets, in which price signals cannot operate to remove either shortages or excesses.

Nixon's gamble

A more recent example of price controls comes from the administration of President Nixon in August 1971. At a time of enormous downward pressure on the US dollar, and equally enormous upward pressure on the rate of US inflation, Nixon suspended convertibility of the US dollar into gold (in effect, ending the Bretton Woods system of fixed but adjustable exchange rates); imposed an import surcharge of 10 per cent, in a bid to protect US producers from foreign competition; and signed Executive Order 11615, thereby imposing a ninety-day freeze on wages and prices, in an effort to counter the inflationary consequences of the other two actions. That, however, was only the beginning of price and wage controls: phase II, which ended in January 1973, required any price or wage increase to be consistent with guidelines imposed by the Cost of Living Council (run by a young and ambitious Donald Rumsfeld) and regulated by the Pay Board and the Price Commission. Large firms – arbitrarily defined – had to gain approval before pushing through any wage or price increase, while small firms had to report increases that went beyond the guidelines. It was, in effect, a bureaucratic mess.

Phase III was associated with a relaxation of price and wage controls. Latent inflationary pressures reappeared with a vengeance, forcing Nixon to impose yet more controls in June 1973, which in turn led to phase IV of the programme. By that stage, however, a combination of bureaucratic inefficiency, free-market arbitrage and hopelessly loose monetary policy had made the controls largely ineffective. Indeed, as a Minneapolis Fed statistical analysis concluded four years later, 'wage and price controls are not likely to provide lasting relief from inflation'.[12] Worse,

> prices were below what they would have been [in the absence of controls] during phases I and II but, except for a brief period, wages were not. Thus, the real wage increased more than it would have, and employment and output dropped. As phase II ended, though, prices began to catch up. Because controls had little effect on wages, this catch-up lowered the real wage, and firms responded by hiring more workers and boosting production.

In other words, the controls may not have had a permanent impact on production, but its volatility increased in the short term, while inflation ended up permanently higher than it might otherwise have been. Not, then, a great example of lasting economic success.

While the Nixon shock proved ultimately to be an economic failure, it appealed to those who thought that inflation was only caused either by nasty events taking place elsewhere in the world (consistent with Nixon's protectionist instincts) or by the activities of (depending on one's political point of view) greedy companies or avaricious unions. Like Harold Wilson's UK experience a handful of years later, the politically attractive option trumped the economically coherent alternative.

Renewed demand for price controls

Almost inevitably, the rapid rise in inflation after the recent Covid-19 pandemic led to renewed calls for price controls of one kind or another. The most obvious justification stemmed from Vladimir Putin's decision to reduce the supply of pipeline natural gas from Russia to the European Union in response to sanctions imposed on Russia for its invasion of Ukraine. Wholesale natural gas prices rose tenfold between the start of 2021 and late 2022, helping to lift inflation to rates not seen since the 1970s and early 1980s. A secondary justification – linked to the central bankers' own claims that rising inflation was 'transitory' and had nothing to do with monetary policy – was that there was no point in raising interest rates to deal with price increases that stemmed from supply shocks, rather than monetary errors.[13]

Two of the more prominent arguments in favour of price controls came courtesy of Isabella Weber from the University of

Massachusetts, Amherst, and Todd Tucker from the Roosevelt Institute.[14] Weber's argument was based on the idea that companies were taking advantage of supply shortages to raise prices, and hence boost profits, consistent with what happened at the end of the Second World War. She suggested that 'the government could target the specific prices that drive inflation instead of moving to austerity which risks a recession'. She went on to claim that there is 'a choice between tolerating the ongoing explosion of profits that drives up prices or tailored controls on carefully selected prices'. Tucker also argued in favour of 'selective price controls' for products which – owing to the impact of Covid on supply chains – were experiencing temporary shortages. He took the view that, in a world of oligopolies and monopolies – in other words, one in which companies are mostly price setters, rather than price takers – it was incumbent upon governments to step in and deliver a fairer outcome for consumers than might otherwise be the case. When restrictions associated with wartime or lockdown are lifted – moments in which supply disruptions of one kind or another are likely – avaricious companies will supposedly raise prices more than necessary, justifying greater government intervention than in other circumstances.

These arguments seem superficially attractive. After all, the end of the pandemic was associated with countless supply shortages. On closer inspection, however, it turns out that the data are not fully consistent with the narrative. First, the corporate profit share in US GDP began its rising trend in around 2000, yet thereafter inflation was mostly in retreat: clearly pricing power is not the only reason why profits can rise. Second, the most profitable sectors within US industry, even as profits increased particularly rapidly over the pandemic period, were those that had the smallest price increases, not the largest. Third, applying 'targeted' or 'selective' controls to deal with inflation is no easy task, if those sectors with the largest price increases are as diverse as furniture, car and truck rental, and hotels and motels, as occurred coming out of the pandemic. Indeed, as inflation spread through the US economy in 2021 and 2022, it became increasingly clear that there was no real case for 'targeted' controls – for the simple reason that the government would end up targeting near enough everything.[15]

This is not to say that controls can never serve a useful purpose. As Hugh Rockoff argued in *Drastic Measures: A history of wage and price controls in the United States*, controls may sometimes reduce the pain associated with a necessarily restrictive set of macroeconomic policies. Importantly, however, 'without monetary restraint, controls will fail'. Indeed, this was one of the key distinctions between the effectiveness of controls during the Korean War (when the Federal Reserve was given the freedom to pursue a restrictive monetary policy) and their ineffectiveness during the Vietnam War (when, for one reason or another, the Federal Reserve chose not to put the monetary brakes on). Moreover, 'controls were most effective when they were applied across the board. When key prices were omitted, demand shifted to those areas, leading to substantial price increases and a distortion in production.' This suggests that there is little chance of success with only selective measures. More generally, while 'the modern state has the power to control prices even in the face of a vast expansion of aggregate demand ... [it] can do so only through a drastic regimentation of economic life' – an outcome that might be acceptable in wartime conditions, but not in most other circumstances, as Harold Wilson's government discovered to its considerable cost in the mid-1970s.[16]

Controlling energy prices

As for energy prices, the case for 'targeted' controls may be politically attractive – indeed, even necessary – but the economic case is, sadly, less secure. None of the available options can easily be made to work, unless any initial increase in energy prices is quickly reversed. That, however, may be wishful thinking. Gas prices, for example, were rising long before Putin's invasion of Ukraine, partly on the back of rapidly rising Chinese demand, as Beijing attempted to replace its dirty coal-fired power stations with cleaner gas-fired equivalents. In effect, the increase in gas prices was initially more a Chinese demand story than it was a Russian gas pipeline supply story.[17]

One option to limit the impact of higher energy prices on inflation would be to impose price ceilings on the energy companies, leaving them unable to pass on increases in wholesale prices to their customers. The consequence would be increased bankruptcy risk – precisely the UK domestic energy providers' experience in late 2021. Another option would be to impose windfall taxes on those standing to gain the most from the energy price increases. Again, the energy companies would find themselves in the firing line. Lowering their post-tax profits, however, might act as a disincentive to invest for the future in non-Russian or non-gas energy alternatives. A third alternative would be to drive a wedge between the gas price paid by domestic or business customers and the wholesale price of gas via subsidies funded by an increase in government borrowing.

This third option sounds remarkably similar to the mixture of furlough and business-support schemes initiated during the Covid pandemic: like those, the aim would be to prevent households or business from ending up in severe financial difficulty and, in extreme cases, bankruptcy. Pandemics, however, tend to run their course, either because the virus mutates or, in the modern era, because a vaccine is found. Energy price hikes, on the other hand, can last a long time: the quadrupling of the price of oil in 1973 was followed by a further doubling in 1979. It wasn't until the mid-1980s that prices came back down again. Energy price subsidies for more than a decade would have carried catastrophic implications for the public finances, reducing the chances of achieving any lasting reduction in inflation. In effect, the impact of higher energy prices would only have been shifted to future taxpayers. And that is assuming that persistent and large government deficits could be funded: as we have already seen, the UK's attempt to support growth in the mid-1970s led only to a collapse in sterling and the eventual arrival of the IMF. Meanwhile, with government borrowing spiralling out of control, the chances of bringing inflation to heel would be increasingly remote. We're back to the Burton–Taylor problem.

There is also a major adding-up challenge. If higher gas prices represent a shortage of gas, and if the impact of a continuous war means there is no near-term prospect of an increase in gas supplies, one country's gas subsidy is, in effect, an act of protectionism against other nations. Its citizens benefit from lower gas prices than elsewhere and thus its economy is likely in the near term to be less badly damaged than others (assuming, of course, that the subsidy can easily be financed). If, however, all countries behave in the same way, there will be no *ex ante* change in the demand for gas: households and businesses will carry on as before. Yet, *ex post*, they cannot carry on, for the simple reason that subsidies do nothing to increase gas supplies. The only possible outcome is a further huge increase in wholesale gas prices, boosting revenues for the malevolent gas producer and, thus, requiring even bigger subsidies from the governments of gas importers.[18] Ultimately, either supply has to increase to meet higher demand – which, in the case of gas, may mean switching from Russian gas pipelines to, say, Qatari supplies, implying the construction of new pipelines or a huge expansion of liquefied natural gas (LNG) shipping and storage facilities, all of which takes time – or else demand has to fall to meet lower supply. Perversely, subsidising energy prices may lead to a particularly bad outcome in the longer term. By weakening the public finances, the Burton–Taylor problem threatens to re-emerge: unless the central bank is prepared to offset fiscal laxity with tough monetary medicine (the sort of thing the Bundesbank excelled at in the 1980s), the risk is that inflation will take off on a more sustained basis. In other words, lower inflation today leads only to higher inflation tomorrow.

Sargent's major problem

Having explained why price ceilings and other forms of 'control' are not likely to be terribly successful in solving an inflationary problem, it's time to return to the expectations debate. Thomas Sargent's observations regarding the end of hyperinflationary traumas have, in a sense, become key parts of the conventional wisdom regarding the setting of monetary policy: central bank independence, fiscal prudence, a commitment to avoid prom-ising too much on either tax cuts or spending increases. If a country has an inflationary problem, give an independent central bank the legal authority to tackle it.[19] If a country has 'fiscal flatulence', come up with a fiscal rule to elicit 'good behaviour' over the medium term. One way or another, that's precisely where most developed nations – and an increasing number of emerging nations – have been since the 1990s.

For many years, the results were impressive. What Sargent didn't tackle, however, is what should be done were inflation to return. It's not possible, after all, to make the central bank independent twice (unless, of course, it lost its independence in between times). Yet, in 2021, as inflation began its seemingly remorseless rise, something had clearly gone wrong. Was Sargent's support for central bank independence misguided? Or, instead, was central bank independence necessary, but in no way sufficient to guarantee lasting price stability? And, if it wasn't, what guarantee was there that inflation would return to target?

The role – supposedly – of expectations

The standard defence used by central bankers is that inflation is unlikely to be a persistent problem, so long as inflationary expectations remain stable. It's not difficult to see why that conclusion was reached. After all, both Friedman and Phelps made expectations a central part of their critique of the Phillips curve, while Lucas and Sargent took the view that the correct institutional framework today could help anchor inflationary expectations for tomorrow and beyond. Since then, measures of inflationary expectations have proliferated far and wide, ranging from those embedded in index-linked (inflation-protected) bond markets through to surveys of businesses, consumers and financial analysts and, most obviously, the large number of formal forecasts concocted by those many economists employed to do such things. Each of these measures can, in theory, be used as a gauge to assess whether monetary policy is on track.

In practice, however, some of these measures may be less than helpful. Take the standard approach adopted by the majority of forecasting economists. Once they know what a central bank's inflation target is, and over what time horizon it is supposed to be achieved, the likelihood is that they will 'forecast' an inflation rate broadly in line with the target at the end of the relevant time horizon. That, however, feels more like an assumption than a forecast (it is a forecast in a formal sense, but it is typically based on an act of faith, not a rigorous analysis of the available data). Lots of things can potentially affect inflation, but for the typical forecasting economist, they are mostly brushed to one side. To be fair, the technique worked remarkably well during the many years of price stability; but the fact that it worked in the past says little about its chances of working in the future. Even as the inflationary dynamic in 2021 was morphing into something not seen for many a decade, forecasts for the next two years barely budged: it was, it seemed, easier to pretend that the past was the best guide to the future, regardless of the emerging inflationary threats. This was, in effect, a repeat of a problem encountered in the late 1960s, when a rudimentary forecasting community persisted with 'mean reversion' forecasts of US inflation, even as actual inflation began its persistent upward movement.

More generally, knowing people's expectations of inflation at any point in time says nothing about how those expectations might change in the future. No one has come up with a decent theory to explain how, at the macroeconomic level, expectations are formed. That, in turn, opens up the possibility that, even though expectations may be important in some conceptual sense, they are little help in gauging where, for example, inflation is ultimately heading.[20] Moreover, the typical economic models in which expectations are incorporated have bizarre properties – at variance with economic reality and sometimes downright implausible – suggesting that the economics profession has yet to get to grips with a topic that is supposedly of the utmost importance.[21]

Rules of thumb and Manchester United

Indeed, and contrary to the alleged properties of *Homo economicus*, most of us probably have only poorly formed expectations, more akin to 'rules of thumb' than carefully calibrated thoughts about the future. We don't worry very much about inflation when it is persistently low, for the simple reason that it does little to distort our perception of economic reality. We do worry, however, when inflation moves higher, because the associated distortions threaten to have a material impact on our livelihoods. During periods of sustainably low inflation, we may happily believe that central banks have got the problem licked. We may begin to revise that view, however, if inflation subsequently reappears.

After all, we do much the same in many other walks of life. Between the 1992/1993 and the 2012/2013 season, Manchester United won the Premier League on thirteen separate occasions, with pundits mostly thinking United's dominance would continue. During the following decade, however, United were seemingly lost in the Premier League wilderness. No longer did competing teams believe United's home ground, Old Trafford, to be impregnable, and no longer were the Red Devils feared by opposition supporters. *Ex post*, there were plenty of available explanations for United's decline: changes in ownership, management and transfer policies. No one, however, suggested that United started losing because, suddenly, its players and supporters began to expect defeats, rather than victories.

The use of rules of thumb – or heuristics, to use a more technical term – is doubtless widespread: it's an easy and efficient way to make sense of the world for much of the time. It is also, however, a source of potential uncertainty. If we occasionally revise our rules, when do we do so, and why? Central banks would be more than happy if the public continuously used a rule of thumb along the lines of 'expect inflation to be equal to target', as Mervyn King, the then-governor of the Bank of England, explained in 2005. If, however, the rule of thumb were to change to, say, 'the central bank is talking tosh, has no ability or inclination to meet the inflation target and actual inflation is likely to rise rapidly', the central bank would find itself in a bit of trouble.

When rules of thumb change

It may take quite a significant shock to change people's rules of thumb; but, as we cannot be sure how those rules are formed in the first place, it is surely incumbent upon central bankers to look for the warning signs regarding people's thoughts about the future. Measures of inflationary expectations, however, are probably the wrong place to start. Expectations rise only because rules of thumb have already changed in response to some other development that triggered a revised worldview. In the case of Manchester United, unexpectedly frequent losses against supposedly inferior teams, together with changes in ownership and management, led to revised rules of thumb regarding Premier League prospects. In the case of central banks, unexpectedly large increases in inflation in 2021 and onwards, and an absence of any immediate or sizeable action to quell price pressures, threatened revised rules of thumb regarding the chances of securing lasting price stability.

This, in turn, creates a significant problem. Imagine central banks are slow to recognise this shift in public perceptions towards a more sceptical, less trusting, attitude. If so, they are likely to offer too little in the way of monetary tightening in response to a rise in inflation, their slow reactions predicated on now-redundant rules of thumb that were based on a previously high level of public trust in the monetary priesthood. Moreover, if central banks provide feeble excuses for any inflationary acceleration – 'it's transitory, it's temporary, it stems from Covid, it reflects an energy price shock' – without genuinely grappling either with the change in public attitudes or with the reality of the new inflationary environment, they could end up in even more trouble. A new rule of thumb might be 'these central bankers don't know what they're doing' – the equivalent of Manchester United fans standing up at Old Trafford and chanting to their owners 'Stand up if you hate the Glazers!'[22]

Fighting inflation: conclusions

A 'policy rules' framework is vital. Monetary policy works better if the public has an idea of what the central bank would do in various different circumstances. The public also needs to know that the monetary framework is not likely to be hijacked by fiscal excess: intuitively, if not rationally, people know there is a Burton–Taylor relationship between monetary and fiscal policy, and it simply isn't credible for policymakers to head off in fundamentally different directions.

The monetary authority must hold sway over the fiscal authority; or, at the very least, monetary policy must dominate fiscal policy. Sargent's hyperinflations came to an end precisely because money financing of budget deficits came to an end. Any whiff of a reversal – most obviously a persistent commitment to quantitative easing – threatens to undermine this simple rule.

Price and wage controls have their place in history and, for that matter, in macroeconomic policy; but that place is very limited, partly because such controls impose unacceptable restrictions on the freedoms we enjoy in peacetime. Importantly, they will only serve a useful purpose (if at all) by buttressing already-tight monetary policies: they are not a substitute for central bank action.

While expectations theoretically matter, their formation is very poorly understood. Most of us use economical 'rules of thumb' to live our daily lives, and only revise them occasionally. Importantly, however, those revisions can fundamentally change how, for example, the monetary authority is perceived. If, in turn, the monetary authority fails to recognise that change in perception, its chances of success in meeting its inflationary target may rapidly decline. Put another way, the worst kind of central bank is the one that complacently believes its own anti-inflation propaganda.

Knowing all this, how should we think about the re-emergence of inflation post-pandemic? Where did it come from? And how might we get rid of it? I next look at what our policymakers got right – and what they got wrong. Anti-inflation propaganda, it turns out, has been far too seductive.

6

Four Inflationary Tests

Squalls and storms – lessons from the 1970s – the problem with inflation targeting – backward-looking Taylor rule – 'time machine' Svensson rules – why central banks need the 'four tests'

Inflationary squalls

One version of recent history is that western nations were simply dealt a dose of bad luck. The reappearance of inflation in 2021 and beyond reflected a series of external shocks beyond any one nation's – or any one central bank's – control. The pandemic triggered temporary supply disruptions. Vladimir Putin's control over Europe's gas supplies led to huge energy price increases in the wake of the war in Ukraine. China's renewed Covid-inspired lockdowns in 2022 undermined global supply chains. All told, the reappearance of inflation reflected no more than a series of unfortunate events. The implication was that inflation would disappear as quickly as it had arrived.

Perhaps it will. There is, after all, precedent for such inflationary squalls. Shortly after the Second World War, the removal of price controls in the US led to a major but short-lived spike in inflation. In 1946 alone, inflation averaged a chunky 18.1 per cent, dropping to a still hefty 8.8 per cent average in 1947. By 1949, however, prices were falling.

These, however, were peculiar circumstances. Wartime rationing had kept prices lower than they would have been in a 'free market', particularly given that wartime was, as usual, associated with both monetary and fiscal stimulus. Having spent their time making armaments, people had money to spend, but rationing in effect prevented them from spending it. With the war at an end, rationing was no longer necessary and, frankly, no longer desirable: it had, after all, helped create a growing black market and an institutionalised acceptance of corruption. Ending rationing simply meant that prices could adjust upwards to where they would have been in its absence.[1]

Another temporary inflationary squall occurred during the 1950–1953 Korean War: inflation of around 6 per cent in the US in both 1950 and 1951 thereafter rapidly petered out, as the conflict turned into a stalemate, leading to the 1953 armistice. Other nations also experienced an inflationary blip. The war's end paved the way to a period of relative tranquillity regarding price pressures.

Squalls can become storms

It's understandably tempting to think that temporary aberrations of this kind are the main cause of inflation in a world in which price stability is the norm. Given the overall loss in the value of money since the collapse of the gold standard in the 1930s, however, it's a temptation that should be resisted. It's the kind of thinking, after all, that got the world into such an inflationary mess in the late 1960s and early 1970s. Here's Anthony Barber, the then-chancellor of the Exchequer, offering his explanation for the rise in inflation in the early 1970s:

> To a considerable extent ... inflation has been the consequence of costs and prices imported from abroad and over which we have no control.[2]

His statement was made in February 1974, shortly after world oil prices had quadrupled. It was easier to blame the Arab oil embargo, a response to the West's perceived support for Israel in the 1973 Yom Kippur War, than to accept that anything had gone wrong domestically in the UK.

The following month, following a change of government, the narrative (perhaps inevitably) changed. Denis Healey, Labour's new chancellor, noted that:

> 1973 saw a rapid growth in money and credit ... money supply, broadly defined, rose by 27 per cent in the past year. The public sector borrowing requirement of over £4 billion was a powerful contributory force in this monetary expansion.[3]

He added that:

> price controls and subsidies, even in alliance with the most perfect incomes policy which could be devised, cannot go far towards winning the battle against inflation if fiscal and monetary policy are pulling in the opposite direction.[4]

In effect, Healey recognised that, while the quadrupling of oil prices was one factor behind the increase in UK inflation, it was not the only factor. Moreover, unlike his predecessor, he was unwilling to pretend that inflation would somehow 'self-correct'. Barber had argued in February 1974 that 'the consequence of the staggering increase in oil prices at present will be to put up prices in this country. The consequence of that will be to depress consumer demand.'[5] Barber was suggesting, in effect, that higher oil prices would ultimately slow the economy. By so doing, he hoped that inflation would automatically come back down again. It did not.

Barber's political instinct was to blame inflation on a series of unfortunate events. Yet, as I've argued throughout this book, inflation cannot be seen purely as a random, event-driven process. Sometimes inflationary shocks fade very quickly. On other occasions, however, they appear either to trigger a sustained wage–price spiral or to add to an already-established inflationary process. Shocks are interesting, but, when it comes to inflation, they are far from being the whole story. Figure 6.1, for example, shows the path for oil prices since the early 1970s, tracked against the US inflation rate. While there have been plenty of oil 'shocks', only some – those in the 1970s and at the time of writing – have been associated with more persistent inflationary woes.

A fundamental problem with inflation targeting

An alternative approach is to consider the broader conditions under which inflationary pressures are likely to be sustained, taking into account institutions, ideas and political economy ambitions. For the 1970s, as I've already noted, the answer is

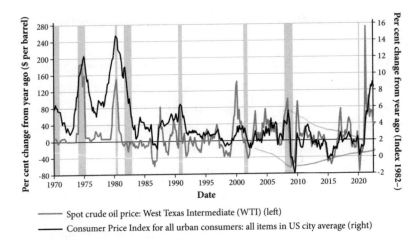

Spot crude oil price: West Texas Intermediate (WTI) (left)

Consumer Price Index for all urban consumers: all items in US city average (right)

Note: Shaded areas indicate US recessions
Source: St Louis Fed; BLS

Figure 6.1: For inflation, some oil price shocks are more shocking than others

relatively easy: the institutional arrangements that had served to 'anchor' inflation broke down; the dollar's convertibility to gold was rescinded, leading to a sustained devaluation; the Bretton Woods system of fixed but adjustable exchange rates disappeared virtually overnight; and there was a collective failure to recognise money's role – in the broadest of senses – in fuelling the inflationary process.

More recently, however, other reasons for a loss of inflationary 'grip' have emerged. From the very beginnings of the inflation-targeting era in the late 1980s, there was an obvious conceptual challenge which, at some point, threatened to become a real-life headache for policymakers. Monetary decisions taken today only affect inflationary outcomes at some unspecified time in the future. Following its operational independence in 1997, the Bank of England quickly concluded that the typical 'lag' was around two years, seemingly in opposition to earlier monetarist claims that lags at all times were 'long and variable'.

This, however, meant that current policy decisions had to be justified on the basis of a 'forecast' for the future, even when that future was highly uncertain. Policymakers ended up in this position not because they were content – how could they be? – but because they had apparently exhausted all other alternatives. In earlier decades, monetary policy had been conducted on the basis that something that could be controlled in the here and now – known as an 'intermediate target' – was predictably linked to the 'ultimate objective' of price stability. Yet intermediate targets mostly didn't do the job for which they had been selected. In musical terms, they were badly off key. They included, most obviously, narrow and broad versions of the monetary aggregates (for which we can thank Milton Friedman et al.) and the exchange rate. Attempts to control these intermediate targets revealed two problems: first, they sometimes misbehaved;[6] and second, their relationship with inflation was, frankly, unstable.[7]

In effect, the move to inflation targeting appeared to reduce the importance of these various 'middlemen'. As time went by, the transmission mechanism of monetary policy (including the various channels through which changes in policy rates feed through to the broader economy) was simply taken for granted. All that mattered, apparently, was the impact of policy changes on people's expectations.

Given the lags involved, what was the best way of gauging the correct monetary stance at any one moment in time? Two approaches emerged, one remarkably simple, yet not terribly forward-looking; and one completely forward-looking, but requiring the use of a time machine.

The Taylor rule: selecting policies with a rear-view mirror

The simple approach, first formulated by John Taylor in 1993,[8] became known as the Taylor rule. This rule was an attempt to characterise not so much what the Federal Reserve *should* do, but rather what it *did* do: to that extent, it was initially a descriptive device, designed to tease out how the Federal Reserve at that time reached its monetary policy decisions. The rule was remarkably simple: the Federal Reserve would raise its policy rate by half a percentage point for each percentage point increase in inflation relative to the Fed's (assumed) 2 per cent target and for each percentage point that output rose relative to its potential (itself one of the vaguest concepts in economics). The rule had both a backward-looking inflationary element (the latest published inflation rate, always released with a lag) and, in theory at least, a forward-looking element, namely the degree to which the economy was operating above capacity. This latter element could be regarded as an indicator of potential future inflationary pressures. In truth, however, such measures of the so-called 'output gap' are not as forward looking as they ideally should be, given the huge revisions they can be subject to in later years.[9]

Those paid to worry about such things routinely used the Taylor rule to work out what the Federal Reserve might do next.[10] Armed with the current inflation rate and a rough assessment regarding the level of demand relative to the available supply, analysts were able to 'guess' where policy rates might be heading. Over time, however, the rule became less effective, in part because the relationship between the real-time estimates of the output gap and future inflation became considerably weaker: put simply, inflation scarcely budged, regardless of whether demand was too strong or too weak. Some policymakers concluded that this changing relationship meant central bank credibility was now higher than ever. The economic cycle apparently no longer played a significant role in determining inflationary outcomes, suggesting a nirvana of unerring price stability. Others feared that a sudden rise in inflation would now be more difficult to eradicate, if, indeed, inflation more generally was impervious to changes in demand.[11]

One version of this rather pessimistic conclusion appeared relatively early. In their seminal 2002 paper on the so-called 'Great Moderation' – a term hijacked thereafter by central bankers keen to burnish their inflation-fighting credentials – two US economists, James Stock and Mark Watson, concluded presciently:

> To the extent that improved policy gets some of the credit, then one can expect at least some of the moderation [in the volatility of output and inflation] to continue as long as the policy regime is maintained. *But because most of the reduction seems to be due to good luck in the form of smaller economic disturbances, we are left with the unsettling conclusion that the quiescence of the past fifteen years could well be a hiatus before a return to more turbulent economic times* [my emphasis].[12]

More prosaically, perhaps, some worried that the Taylor rule was becoming less useful, for the simple reason that it appeared to suggest that monetary policy should adjust primarily in response to past inflation misses. This was a distinctly uncomfortable conclusion, suggesting that those responsible for 'driving' the economy were doing so using only the rear-view mirror. No one would drive a car that way. Why would policymakers do so?

The 'forward-looking rule': fine if you have a time machine

This led to the rather more complicated 'forward-looking approach' espoused by, among others, Lars Svensson, and commonly referred to as 'forecast targeting'.[13] Svensson himself summarised the approach as follows:

(i) For a given policy rate path (for example, the policy rate path from the previous decision), construct new inflation and unemployment forecasts, taking into account new information received since the previous decision.

(ii) If the new inflation and unemployment forecasts 'look good' (meaning that they best fulfill the mandate), select the given policy rate path as the decision; if the new inflation and unemployment forecasts do not look good, adjust the policy rate path so that they do look good.

(iii) Publish the policy rate path and inflation and unemployment forecasts and justify the decision in order to make the published path and forecasts credible, meaning making market participants' and other economic agents' expectations align with the published path and forecasts. The justification of the decision may include the publication of inflation and unemployment forecasts for alternative policy rate paths different from the selected one and the demonstration that these forecasts do not fulfill the mandate to the same degree.[14]

While this approach is now widely embraced by the world's central banks, a moment's thought reveals a rather obvious weakness. Driving an economy is not like driving a car. When driving a car, the information gathered from what's in front of the windscreen is both current and hopefully accurate, allowing the driver to adjust both the steering and the car's speed, in response to the challenges typically experienced on a journey. Svensson's approach is akin to making crucial decisions about tomorrow's journey today, setting the wheels in motion for a trip based on predicted, rather than actual, obstacles. It's the sort of journey that most of us would prefer to avoid, unless, that is, a time machine is handily available.

To be fair, Svensson's approach does have a 'feedback' loop, but it cannot possibly distinguish between periods during which inflation increases only temporarily and those when inflation threatens to shift to a permanently higher rate. In real time, it's difficult to spot the difference. If the lag between changes in interest rates and inflation is, say, two years, any feedback gleaned from one month to the next will be of negligible value, unless that feedback includes, for example, changes that say something meaningful about the world at least two years hence. Central bankers often suggest that stable expectations might offer reassurance; but, as I argued in chapter 5, inflationary expectations themselves tend only to change with a lag. Put another way, relying on 'feedback' cannot offer much in the way of help during periods in which a shift from low to high inflation – or vice versa – might be taking place. The feedback simply comes too late, the equivalent of waiting until there is a head-on collision to realise that, yes, something might have been done earlier to avoid the accident: interesting in hindsight, perhaps, but utterly useless in real time.

The difference between a simple Taylor rule and a 'forecast targeting' rule only serves to reveal the extent to which, in the light of the pandemic and subsequent energy price shocks, central bankers entered a world of apparent confusion and bewilderment. While the Taylor rule suggested that policy rates should have been increasing rapidly to counter a rise in actual inflation, the 'forecast targeting' rule suggested quite the opposite, based on the idea that any near-term inflationary disturbance carried few, if any, inflationary implications for the future. Indeed, even as actual inflation persistently surprised on the upside, central bankers' inflation forecasts barely moved.

Helpfully, the Atlanta Fed provides a webpage that allows those interested in the Taylor rule (in all its many permutations) to compare actual policy rates – driven primarily by variations of the 'forecast targeting' rule – with what the Taylor rule might suggest.[15] From the moment inflation started rising in 2021, the gap between the two 'rules' widened dramatically. In the second quarter of 2022, for example, the actual US policy rate was a little under 1 per cent. Three variations of the Taylor rule suggested that the policy rate should have been anywhere between 5.5 and 7.5 per cent, the highest since the 1980s. The gap between the two inflation-targeting methodologies was now a canyon. Having abandoned the Taylor rule, central bankers were, in effect, pretending to have a time machine that allowed them to confirm that today's inflation carried few implications for inflation in two years' time. Yet how could they possibly know?

The answer, apparently, was that deviations from target could only be temporary in nature, because the public recognised the central banks' ultimate monetary infallibility. Central bankers were often happy to encourage such beliefs, partly by emphasising the 'temporary' nature of inflation shocks (in a clear echo of the complacent attitudes witnessed in the early 1970s). Ben Broadbent, a deputy governor at the Bank of England, offered the following thoughts at the tail end of 2021:

There's a good chance that this [price of traded goods] shock too, larger though it is, will have dissipated by the time a policy decision taken now could take effect. Indeed it's quite possible that, in a couple of years, some of these tradable goods prices will be falling, pulling down on inflation.[16]

Five months later, after another Covid lockdown in China and Russia's invasion of Ukraine, Broadbent's boss, Andrew Bailey, the governor of the Bank of England, gave his view:

It's a very, very difficult place to be. To forecast 10 per cent inflation and to say there isn't a lot we can do about it is an extremely difficult place to be ... This is a bad situation to be in. A sequence of shocks like this, which have come really one after another with no gaps between them, is almost unprecedented.[17]

He was, in effect, arguing that near-term inflation was beyond the bank's control, but would likely have little impact on inflation further out. In effect, 'stuff happens'. Over the medium term, inflation will apparently stay low, because the central banks assume our faith in them is unwavering. Yet this falls foul of Mervyn King's 'King Canute' theory of inflation: in his words, 'a satisfactory theory of inflation cannot take the form "inflation will remain low because we say it will"'.[18]

The post-pandemic inflationary shock

Stuff certainly does happen, but the big challenge regarding inflation is to work out which of its many instances are temporary – the Korean War, for example – and which are likely to persist. Put another way, how is it possible to tell in real time whether an inflation problem is serious or otherwise?

In my view, any answer must involve what I call the 'four tests':

- Test 1: have there been any institutional changes suggesting an increased bias in favour of inflation?
- Test 2: have there been signs of monetary excess sufficient to indicate a heightened inflationary risk?
- Test 3: is there evidence to suggest that a rising inflationary risk is being trivialised, notably through 'time machine' or 'external shock' arguments?
- Test 4: have supply-side conditions changed for the worse?

Test 1: Inflation-threatening institutional change

In the run-up to the pandemic and all that happened thereafter, the simple answer is 'yes', there was inflation-threatening institutional change. Consider three of the arguments from earlier in the book:

- The bias against *deflation* may have inadvertently created a bias in favour of *inflation*. Indeed, the Federal Reserve's August 2020 shift to a 'flexible average inflation target' (FAIT) almost guaranteed such an outcome. Any large inflationary overshoots would be difficult to offset with future inflationary undershoots, given an inflation target of 2 per cent and fears that inflation lower than 2 per cent might require interest rates to bump into the so-called zero lower bound, triggering a much-feared bout of deflation.[19] In other words, FAIT created a dynamic in favour of a higher average inflation rate than the official 2 per cent target, because the public knew both that central banks would not tolerate inflation persistently below the 2 per cent target and that central banks would tolerate – and, at the time of writing this book, were tolerating – inflation well above the 2 per cent target.

- The commitment to quantitative easing removed one of the key early-warning indicators – freely moving prices in government bond markets – used by central banks to gauge inflationary risks. It was the equivalent of dismantling radar stations based on an assumption that there would be no more enemy bombing raids: by implication, future attacks would be spotted only once the enemy planes were directly overhead, an utterly useless approach. Quantitative easing had also reduced the discipline imposed on fiscal policymakers. Although central bankers would doubtless claim it as mere coincidence, it's striking that an extended period of quantitative easing was associated with the biggest ever peacetime increase in government debt. Would government debt have risen quite as far without being 'underwritten' by central banks? Would finance ministries have been quite so generous in their fiscal largesse, had they had to contend with the risk of significantly higher debt interest payments in the absence of quantitative easing?

- Central bank independence appeared to break the institutionalised version of the link – the Burton–Taylor relationship – between monetary and fiscal policy. With monetary independence, it was convenient to claim that fiscal policy had no bearing on inflationary outcomes – a very useful result for governments keen to free themselves from the shackles of monetary discipline. This was, ultimately, the justification used by Kwasi Kwarteng, the newly appointed – and remarkably short-lived – chancellor of the Exchequer, when he announced huge tax cuts in the UK in September 2022. Equally, central banks could absolve themselves of blame for any fiscal misdemeanours. The absence of proper coordination between the macro levers, however, left policy inherently unstable. Reflecting a fear of lost 'independence', central banks tended to keep quiet even when significant fiscal stimulus was on offer, reluctant to spell out the interest-rate and exchange-rate implications of fiscal excess. Indeed, regarding the monetary implications of fiscal decisions, many central bankers appeared to be engaged in self-censorship, an odd kind of independence.[20]

While each of these developments may have made sense in an environment of persistently low inflation, none of them made sense in a world in which inflation was the bigger risk. Put another way, the overwhelming focus on deflationary threats led to a wholesale adjustment of institutional arrangements, in the process introducing a dangerous asymmetry at the heart of policymaking.

Other institutional changes also occurred. The move away from monetary targets towards pure inflation targeting led to a lack of focus on the various monetary aggregates that, in the late 1970s and 1980s, had been the beating heart of monetary policymaking. True, the relationship between these aggregates and ultimate macroeconomic objectives was, to say the least, imprecise, but the idea that they contained no information at all was surely wrong. While monetary aggregates were hopeless in providing 'precision-engineered' inflation forecasts from one year to the next – with central banks instead placing their faith in time machines – they were nevertheless useful in indicating a possible shift in overall inflationary conditions (as, indeed, anyone familiar with economic history would have known).

Meanwhile, because inflation was seen to be dead, central banks were given multiple objectives that, frankly, would never have been credible in periods of high inflation, when a single-minded determination to restore price stability was paramount. Financial stability, full employment, 'green' finance and, in the European Central Bank's case, preservation of the euro may all have been worthy objectives, but there was no guarantee that they could all be met simultaneously. The inevitable trade-offs forced central banks to make choices that they were politically ill-equipped to carry out.

Test 2: Signs of monetary excess

Monetary excess reveals itself in many ways. Sometimes it emerges in the form of asset price inflation. Think, for example, of the dot-com bubble in the late 1990s or the US housing bubble a few years later. In both cases, balance sheets inflated, leverage rose, central banks tightened monetary policy and the whole thing eventually went 'pop'.

Oddly, asset price inflation need not give rise to more generalised inflation. Indeed, as I argued in 1999 at the tail end of the dot-com bubble,[21] asset price inflation can take off precisely because there is no generalised inflation: it is inflation's absence that creates the illusion that an economy has entered some kind of 'new paradigm', where economic growth appears to be permanently higher even as inflation remains quiescent. The consequent 'rerating' of asset values creates financial riches that typically exceed the economy's capabilities. Those riches, in turn, generate leverage far beyond what can be justified by economic fundamentals. When the central bank eventually applies the monetary brakes – as the Federal Reserve did both in the late 1920s and in 2000 – expectations implicit within stretched asset price valuations typically implode. As they do so, asset prices collapse, leaving a legacy of excessive and indigestible debt. With deleveraging accelerating and demand collapsing, deflation becomes a major threat.

Arguably, such episodes reflect a failure on behalf of central banks to raise 'real' interest rates to the appropriate level when expectations regarding future financial returns are unusually inflated. If life really is as good as asset markets suggest, the discount rate on future investments ought to be more bracing. In other words, available funds should not be frittered away on wasteful projects. Too often, however, central banks ignore this maxim, concluding instead that interest rates can remain low because inflation itself is under control. On some occasions, the result is a housing bubble, as occurred during the US subprime boom in the mid-2000s. On other occasions, the result is investment in poorly understood financial instruments, whose only advantage is their ability in the near term to defy gravity. Good examples include some of the asset price gains witnessed during the 1720 South Sea Bubble, some of the dot-com bubble gains of the late 1990s and, with nominal interest rates at rock-bottom levels after the Global Financial Crisis, the surge in interest in Bitcoin and other crypto currencies.

Periods of genuinely high and sustained inflation – as opposed to inflated expectations about future economic growth – are typically associated with rapid money supply growth, consistent with the conclusions reached by Friedman and Schwartz. US monetary growth exceeded 9 per cent for the first time in the post-war period in 1968, mirroring the rise in inflation at that time. Further, bigger, monetary spurts occurred in spring 1971 (with growth in the so-called M2 monetary aggregate reaching a peak of 13.4 per cent later that year) and in both 1976 and 1977. After occasional monetary upsets in the first half of the 1980s, monetary growth thereafter slowed to a trickle. There were occasional policy-induced 'emergency expansions' – including a spurt in response to the collapse in Lehman Brothers in September 2008 – but, for the most part, it seemed that monetary growth was no longer an issue to worry about.

That all changed in early 2020. As economic activity collapsed alongside Covid-induced lockdowns, central bankers feared a repeat of the 1930s Great Depression, and thus did not consider inflation to be any kind of serious threat. Those fears were reflected in comments through both 2020 and much of 2021, by which time inflation was already heading higher. For example,

> a reduction in office use could ... weigh persistently on demand for rental space and rents, which may feed through into lower cost inflation and a period of weaker price inflation.[22]

Or,

> so far [inflation] seems a pretty negligible risk ... to be sure ... recovery may create some temporary supply-side frictions that could lift costs and prices for a period ... However, I think it is likely that, provided inflation expectations remain contained, the background of ample labour market slack and subdued activity levels will keep a lid on labour costs and margins ... Or, to put it a different way, when considering risks of persistent above-target inflation before we have recovered most of the lost ground, my attitude is I will believe it if and when I see it.[23]

Or,

with the economy and the labour market running so far
below its medium-term potential, we will ultimately need
to close that gap to get inflation sustainably back to target.[24]

Or,

longer-term inflation expectations have moved much less
than actual inflation or near-term expectations, suggesting
that households, businesses and market participants also
believe that the current high inflation readings are likely to
prove transitory and that, in any case, the Fed will keep
inflation close to our 2 percent objective over time.[25]

Few, however, pointed to what was a truly remarkable acceleration in monetary growth. At the beginning of 2020, the annual
rate of growth in US M2 was a modest 6.8 per cent. By May,
monetary growth had exceeded 20 per cent, on its way to an
astonishing 26.8 per cent peak in February 2022. Thereafter,
the monetary expansion slowed, but the damage had already
been done. In effect, the stock of money had risen hugely in a
relatively short space of time. And, for much of that time,
people were unable to spend, owing to the effects of lockdowns.

The rapidity of the monetary expansion contributed, in turn,
to financial outcomes fundamentally different from those experienced during the 1930s Great Depression. Banks survived,
rather than failed. Equity markets roared, rather than collapsed.
Workers were furloughed, not sacked (or, if they were sacked,
they returned to work remarkably quickly). Most businesses
stayed open, while few went under. And, in time, inflation
picked up.

Not all countries and regions experienced such rapid monetary growth. In the eurozone, the favoured M3 monetary aggregate reached double digits towards the end of 2021, nothing like the pace seen in the US. Nevertheless, this was still the fastest rate of expansion in around thirteen years. The UK experience was roughly similar. As with the US, inflation in both cases began to surprise on the upside, relative to consensus forecasts. And, as lockdowns ended, money velocity picked up: suddenly, the earlier increase in what had been 'idle' money balances could be put to good use. Put another way, even as M slowed, V picked up, boosting PT. The quantity theory, in distorted form, was back.

Test 3: Inflationary risks trivialised or 'excused'?

The monetary policy of time machines – or 'forecast targeting' – is susceptible to biased belief systems. If central bankers have mostly worried about the risks of deflation, it is quite difficult for them to adjust their views to a new economic reality fundamentally different from the past.

Comments made during the pandemic and the later energy shock strongly support the idea that any evidence in favour of sustainably rising inflation was, for too long, brushed to one side. The reasons for this included well-behaved inflationary expectations, an unwillingness to focus on the monetary drivers of inflation, an inability to understand the full effects of the pandemic, and a theological faith in the idea that central bankers really were masters of their inflationary universe.

This was not the central bankers' finest hour. Sociologists and psychologists will doubtless have their own views as to the development of 'groupthink' within these hallowed institutions; but perhaps the biggest fault was a refusal to acknowledge that inflation could possibly return on the central bankers' own watch. If, indeed, inflation was back, its resurrection would require central bankers to come to terms with what might appear to be a collective failure. Their job was to deliver price stability, as defined by the inflation target. They couldn't quite bring themselves to accept that they were no longer monetary gods and that, perhaps, they were fallible humans, like the rest of us.[26]

This refusal to accept that the world might have changed led to an ever-lengthening parade of excuses for why rising inflation had nothing to do with monetary policy and, importantly, why any inflationary increase was likely to prove temporary. The time machine, it turned out, could only travel to an inflationary nirvana: apparently, no other destination was possible. Wage–price spirals were for the 1970s, not for the present day: any labour market tightness would quickly be resolved. Energy shocks could only be transitory, and any ripple effects through the broader economy would be short lived. China might be economically 'offline' because of repeated lockdowns, but global supply chains played no sustained role in the formation of inflation. And even if near-term inflation had risen, monetary policy was always set to guarantee that inflation would most likely return to its target within two years.

Table 6.1 provides one version of this story. Taken from successive Bank of England Monetary Policy Reports, it shows how a systematic increase in both current and 'one-year-ahead' inflation had no impact on inflation projections further out (apart from, oddly, November 2022, when the bank signalled an inflationary 'undershoot' in two years' time – an attempt to flag up that financial markets were perhaps too pessimistic about the future level of policy rates). Either central bankers had perfectly calibrated time machines, or they had their heads stuck firmly in the sand.

Table 6.1: Bank of England Monetary Policy Report inflation projections

Date of report	Latest inflation	One-year-ahead inflation	Two-year-ahead inflation
August 2020	0.3	1.8	2.0
November 2020	0.6	2.1	2.0
February 2021	0.8	2.1	2.1
May 2021	1.7	2.3	2.0
August 2021	2.7	3.3	2.1
November 2021	4.3	3.4	2.2
February 2022	5.7	5.2	2.1
May 2022	9.1	6.6	2.1
August 2022	9.9	9.5	2.0
November 2022	10.9	5.5	1.4

Source: Successive Bank of England Monetary Policy Reports

Test 4: Worsening 'supply' conditions

Recall that the Taylor rule required an estimate of the amount of 'slack' within the economy. The so-called output gap – one of the least reliable metrics in the economist's diagnostic kit – is supposed to gauge the degree to which demand is above or below supply. Most central banks calculate this gap as a matter of routine. Some even publish their estimates – an act of bravery, given the likelihood of copious future revisions. Typically, the 'supply-side' performance of an economy is treated as a 'given', something over which monetary policy has no real influence. On that basis, a central bank's main role is to manipulate demand to make sure that the economy is neither 'too hot' nor 'too cold'.

 Supply, however, can vary. One way to show this is via average growth rates from one cyclical peak or trough to the next (Table 6.2). It's a way of adjusting for the variability of demand through the course of each economic cycle. Doing so

Table 6.2: Real economic growth between US cyclical peaks

Peak-to-peak date	Average annualised growth rate (per cent)
1948Q4–1953Q2	5.5
1953Q2–1957Q3	2.5
1957Q3–1960Q2	2.9
1960Q2–1969Q4	4.5
1969Q4–1973Q4	3.7
1973Q4–1980Q1	2.9
1980Q1–1981Q3	1.4
1981Q3–1990Q3	3.4
1990Q3–2001Q1	3.3
2001Q1–2007Q4	2.6
2007Q4–2019Q4	1.7
2019Q4–	1.0

Note: The latest figure extends to the second quarter of 2022
Sources: NBER, St Louis Fed FRED

demonstrates clearly that, far from being a given, supply potential can vary enormously. Notably, since the Global Financial Crisis and the pandemic, US economic growth was far weaker than it had been in earlier episodes.

In real time, it's impossible to know an economy's precise supply potential. Much depends on 'unknowns', such as the rate of technological progress, the degree of labour force participation and the competitive nature of rivals elsewhere in the world. This, in turn, means that monetary errors are still possible. Deflation becomes more likely in circumstances where supply is plentiful, yet demand is depressed. Inflation, by contrast, is more likely when supply is limited, but demand is robust. And those are precisely the conditions that emerged in the aftermath of the pandemic: as some, but not all, economies unlocked, demand was locally robust, even as supply was both locally and globally constrained. The global supply limitations were, in most cases, obvious: China's 'zero-tolerance' Covid protocols, for example, led to repeated lockdowns, even as demand in parts of the developed world surged.

The local supply limitations were, perhaps, a little less clear, but they contributed to roughly the same effects: workers who refused to return to their place of work on the same terms as before; people who opted for early retirement, helped in their choice by booming asset markets; those who chose to stay in their home nation, rather than cross borders in search of more productive employment; the market's failure to recognise and thus respond to growing shortages during the period of lockdown; and, for the UK, a sudden reduction in the 'stretchiness' of the labour market as Brexit slowed the influx of EU workers.

These localised effects showed up most obviously in labour market data. In effect, there were too few workers to meet the needs of a post-pandemic jobs market. Vacancies surged as unemployment tumbled. Nominal wage growth began to accelerate (even if the initial acceleration was dwarfed by rapidly rising headline inflation, mostly reflecting rapid increases in energy prices). Workers began to hop from job to job in pursuit of higher wages. Companies, in turn, began to contemplate offering higher pay, in a bid to retain staff. Unions became increasingly agitated, with days lost through strike action rising rapidly in some countries.

Admittedly, economic growth was hardly robust. To conclude, however, that there was a lack of demand was a fundamental mistake – a repeat, in many ways, of the misinterpretations of the 1970s. Instead, supply was less able to meet demand than previous estimates of 'productive potential' had suggested. It was a bit like discovering that, having avoided the gym for many months, one's ability to lift weights had significantly declined:

trying to lift too much in such circumstances is only likely to lead to injury, visits to the local physiotherapist and, thereafter, a long period of rehabilitation.

Underneath all this, however, was a broader issue pre-dating both the pandemic and Putin's invasion of Ukraine. Recall the words of Stock and Watson cited earlier in this chapter: *'most of the reduction [in inflation] seems to be due to good luck in the form of smaller economic disturbances ...'.* One way of interpreting this is in the context of globalisation. As borders fell and barriers to economic engagement withered, so economic efficiency – as conventionally measured – improved hugely. With capital able to move across borders in search of the most attractive mix of wages, productivity, governance, logistics and rule of law, the price of manufactured goods tumbled. This was, in effect, a repeat of late-nineteenth-century deflationary trends. Admittedly, those employed in manufacturing in relatively high-cost parts of the world – North America, Western Europe – lost out, but they were already relatively few: thanks in part to earlier technological innovations associated with mass automation, there had already been a decisive shift away from jobs in manufacturing to those in the service sector.

These improvements in the global allocation of resources were a big part of what might best be described as a disinflationary supply-side revolution. For central bankers operating in North America and Western Europe, it was a godsend. The ability to hit a given inflation target became so much easier. In effect, there was an extraordinarily favourable tailwind.

In the years following the Global Financial Crisis, however, the first signs began to appear that the earlier era of hyper-globalisation might be ending. Rather than witnessing the emergence of one big, happy family of like-minded democracies, it appeared instead that the world's superpowers – and their satellites – were pulling away from each other. The initial fault line was between the US and China, two remarkably successful economies with fundamentally different political systems. Even before Donald Trump's presidency – four years in which 'America First' became an anti-China mantra – the US Congress had already shifted from regarding China as a partner to regarding it as a threat. Quite simply, Washington had given up on earlier hopes that Beijing might go the same way as Tokyo and Seoul in embracing democratic principles. Beijing, meanwhile, had no great enthusiasm for a world order that was, in effect, 'Made in America'. If China was about to become the world's biggest economy, surely its enhanced gravitational pull required a much bigger voice in international affairs?

Covid simply turbocharged a process of separation that was already under way. Global supply chains, which had previously been regarded as sources of economic efficiency, were now seen as sources of national vulnerability. International organisations that had once been trusted to set the rules of the game – the World Health Organization, for example – were now greeted with suspicion by those who feared that they had become mouthpieces for a particular country's point of view. The speed at which the virus had spread promoted a sense that borders could be a force for good, not merely a cause of unwelcome separation.

Russia's invasion of Ukraine prompted similar soul-searching. Thanks to the construction of the Nord Stream 1 and 2 pipelines, Europe had become strategically dependent on Russian gas supplies. There was no immediately viable alternative. When, therefore, Vladimir Putin decided to turn the taps down, if not quite off, gas prices surged, prompting a European-wide energy crisis. Suddenly, the apparently most efficient source of energy had become a source of enormous vulnerability.

These developments led to a reduction in enthusiasm for globalisation and a renewed focus on what might best be described as 'national resilience'. It was the equivalent of discovering that ownership of a house required insurance to cover unexpected or unforeseen crises: providing security and peace of mind is, it turns out, a costly business. Supply chains were shortened, accelerating a process of 'nearshoring'; companies had to think long and hard about where they chose to invest; and workers no longer moved across borders quite so freely. Put another way, global supply conditions deteriorated, implying that, for any given level of demand, inflation was likely to be higher than it had been previously. This was Stock and Watson's Great Moderation in reverse. To paraphrase: 'some of the increase [in inflation] seems to be due to bad luck in the form of larger economic and political disturbances ...'.

Time machines and tackling inflation: conclusions

In truth, the current inflation rate carries little information about the future inflation rate. Or put another way, the future inflation rate is determined by a host of factors not included within the current inflation rate. To the extent that the future inflation rate was close to the current inflation rate, central bank policy may have played a role; but equally, there is a good chance that the apparent stability between present and future was a matter of good luck, rather than good judgement.

"Right for wrong reason"

As such, it is very difficult in real time to tell the difference between an inflationary squall and a lasting period of inflationary stress. Now that the use of intermediate targets has (understandably) been abandoned, a large element of guesswork is involved in working out where inflation will be two or three years down the road. Expectations don't cut it, for reasons outlined in earlier chapters. Neither, however, do the standard rules governing the making of policy decisions, including both the Taylor rule and the 'forward-looking' rule.

Given the absence of a workable time machine, a better way of assessing inflationary risk is to consider four tests, specifically: (i) have there been any institutional changes suggesting an increased bias in favour of inflation?; (ii) have there been signs of monetary excess sufficient to indicate a heightened inflationary risk?; (iii) is there evidence to suggest that a rising inflationary risk is being trivialised, notably through 'time machine' or 'external shock' arguments?; and (iv) have supply-side conditions changed for the worse?

On all four tests, the rise in inflation during and after the Covid pandemic has been the most worrying since the 1970s. Those who seek to trivialise the increase have, in my view, misunderstood the nature of the threat.

a warning ...

7

Lessons, Warnings and Possible Next Steps

Fourteen lessons – Burton–Taylor revisited – central bank independence when inflation is high – tackling 'groupthink' – avoiding 'one-way bets' – protection against inflationary uncertainty – Burns and Volcker

We have been on an inflationary journey, a voyage that has involved historical evidence, inflationary theories (some good, some less so), methods of inflationary control (some effective, some not so) and, importantly, a huge chunk of political economy. The idea that inflation is neutral, unimportant and thus scarcely worth worrying about can only be described as nonsense. Equally ridiculous is the idea that inflation can ever be permanently defeated. Even when it appears to have been driven to the furthest recesses of our minds, and into the least accessible corners of our institutional memories, it always threatens to return. It offers the economic equivalent of Hollywood's *Terminator*. 'I'll be back' is the shared mantra.

This final chapter splits naturally into two parts. First, I offer fourteen lessons, distilled from the earlier chapters and based not just on theory, but also on the history of inflationary experience. Second, I consider our inflationary futures in terms of the risks, the possible solutions and the institutional constraints. In short, I fear we are entering a new era, in which lasting price stability can no longer be guaranteed.

But first the lessons . . .

Lesson 1: Money matters

Perhaps this is the most important lesson of all. On one level, it's tautologous, because inflation can be seen either as a process by which prices and wages persistently rise, or alternatively, as a process by which the value of money persistently declines. Yet the historical evidence strongly suggests a causal – if admittedly imprecise – link that runs from money to prices, rather than the other way round. While experiments with monetary targeting have failed – partly because they claimed far too much in terms of a precise relationship between money and prices – policymakers must absolutely be cognisant of periods when monetary growth accelerates unusually rapidly. During the pandemic and its aftermath, they were not. Admittedly, there are occasions when inflation surges for 'non-monetary' reasons; but its persistence thereafter still, ultimately, depends on monetary factors: if monetary policy 'accommodates' the price increase, a sustained period of inflation is then more likely: one reason why the UK's inflationary record in the mid-1970s was so much worse than West Germany's.

Lesson 2: Public attitudes matter as much as central bank policies

Pure monetarists tend to believe that money's 'velocity' is stable, or at least predictable. History suggests otherwise, partly because it reveals the importance of public 'trust' in money. Those policymakers who lose the public's trust – Romans who debased silver coinage, French Revolutionaries who introduced new-fangled *assignats*, central bankers who ignore an inflationary threat and choose, complacently, to believe in their own anti-inflation credibility – can trigger untold inflationary damage even when money supply itself is not initially growing at a rampant pace.

Lesson 3: Those who believe inflation has been permanently tamed ignore history

Economic models are typically based on limited data samples. They are mostly constructed to 'fit' recent history. If that history has been one of price stability, then the model is likely to project such stability into the future, regardless of the historical evidence to the contrary. Such model 'complacency', however, is a big mistake: in effect, history tells us that such models are unstable over time and cannot be relied upon during times of political and economic stress.

After three or four decades of price stability, it was easy for people to believe that the future – even in the wake of a pandemic – would bring 'more of the same'. Inflation, however, is a stealthy adversary – a product as much of the realities of political economy as of the technical competence of central bankers. The past can sometimes be a good guide to the future, but only if the policymaker knows where to look. Meanwhile, central bank independence does not provide an absolute guarantee of lasting price stability: those who think it does need to re-examine history.

Lesson 4: Governments can and will resort to inflation

Inflation is a mechanism that rewards debtors, even as it punishes creditors. As one of the biggest such debtors in any economy is typically the government, inflation can be a 'useful' way out of an otherwise impossible fiscal situation: if the public is unwilling to accept either tax increases or spending cuts to 'balance the fiscal books', inflation can achieve a similar result. Put another way, monetary policy alone cannot easily control inflation: it needs to be buttressed by fiscal policy one way or another. Ignoring this 'Burton–Taylor' relationship is asking for trouble.

Lesson 5: Institutional reforms in a world of deflationary risk can lead to an inadvertent bias in favour of inflation

If the future is highly uncertain, it makes little sense to pretend that the 'only' threat is deflation, a world of falling prices and rising real indebtedness. Yet this is precisely what happened in the years between the Global Financial Crisis and the Covid pandemic. Emergency monetary measures such as quantitative easing became seemingly permanent features of the policy-making landscape, reducing the ability of government bond markets, for example, to provide 'early-warning signals' of a potential future inflationary uptick. The problem was made worse in the eurozone, where the European Central Bank was forced to worry less about inflation and more about the risk of ultimate euro break-up, leading to a blurring of the lines between monetary policy and what was in danger of becoming a monetary-driven 'quasi-'fiscal policy.

Lesson 6: Democratically elected governments cannot help but be tempted by inflation

Of the many weaknesses associated with Modern Monetary Theory, perhaps the most striking is the idea that democratically elected governments can be trusted, on their own, to look after the value of money. The case for operationally independent central banks is that they are less likely to fall into temptations associated with the electoral cycle and, in extreme cases, a lack of fiscal 'depth'. The printing press is a temptation precisely because it is an alternative to tax increases or spending cuts, a stealthy way in the short run of robbing people of their savings, particularly given the predilection of policymakers to blame inflation on 'forces beyond their control'. Ultimately, there is no escaping 'Burton–Taylor'.

Lesson 7: Once established, inflation is a deeply unfair and undemocratic process

Simply put, inflation arbitrarily creates both winners and losers. It may be that an economy might perform well in aggregate, at least for a while, but inflation is a deeply corrosive process that ultimately breeds mistrust in society. Few, if any, democracies have been able to cope with inflationary persistence: eventually, the public demands change. The longer the inflation persists, however, the more painful the eventual policy fixes are likely to be. The unfairness is not just about the lags that inevitably exist between price and wage increases. Some will be able to receive wage compensation, while others will be trapped on fixed or only slowly adjusting nominal incomes. The financially sophisticated may be in a better position than others to protect – or expand – their existing wealth. The indebted may benefit, while those with mostly cash savings – poor pensioners, for example – may suffer. Some will benefit from inflation 'indexation', while others will lack any kind of protection.

Lesson 8: Protecting people's incomes and wealth in the light of price shocks may be politically necessary, but such actions rarely solve an inflation problem

If the root cause of persistent inflation is inappropriately loose monetary conditions, then no level of subsidies is going to solve the problem. An enlightened government might be able to anticipate winners and losers from inflation and offer some form of compensation to those who lose out; but the chances are that such a process will be 'captured' by the politically noisy. Far better, therefore, to address inflation's underlying causes than to support those who are able to jostle their way to the front of the queue even as others are left behind. The same goes for price and wage controls: they may help augment an inflation-busting monetary framework, but they should not be regarded as an alternative.

Lesson 9: Hyperinflations, ironically, may be easier to reduce than 'modest' inflations

During hyperinflations, very few benefit in the long run. The vast majority will demand action, making institutional reform ultimately inevitable, even if it happens after a revolution or two. In the final analysis, history suggests the need for an independent central bank and the removal of any hint of fiscal dominance, in order to guarantee that in future, holding money will be a reliable process and not something that leads to huge financial losses. Modest inflations, in contrast, are easier to 'explain away' via external shocks, transitory disturbances and so on. They can, as a result, become more embedded. Their removal is tricky, because the costs of doing so are often, in the near term, regarded as excessive.

Lesson 10: A 'rules-based' policy framework is important: the public need to know how policymakers are likely to respond

Rules help because they create a framework in which people can anticipate what is likely to happen policy-wise as the economy evolves. In the event of, say, a powerful acceleration in economic growth or an unexpected and persistent rise in inflation, it is better for all concerned if the central bank adopts – and is seen to adopt – a bias in favour of higher short-term policy rates. If the government decides to go down a path of inflation-threatening fiscal stimulus, it is useful to know that a significant monetary response will likely be forthcoming.[1] As people's perceptions regarding the policy outlook shift, so the financial markets will be repriced, in effect doing some of the heavy lifting that would otherwise be the responsibility of the monetary authority alone.

Lesson 11: There must be monetary dominance over fiscal policy, not the reverse: the government should not be in the business of 'printing money' to fund its borrowing

What is now known as 'fiscal dominance' has had a long and varied history. Debasing the currency is, after all, a way in which kings and queens would pay for wars by making those with gold and silver coins worse off. The gold standard was one version of monetary dominance, a straitjacket that prevented governments from borrowing at will – until, that is, wartime forced them to. During peacetime, however, governments should ideally be dissuaded from going down the path of printing money to fund budget deficits. Inadvertently, quantitative easing may have paved the way for fiscal dominance 'via the back door'.

Lesson 12: 'Rules of thumb' are more important than expectations

Central bankers are obsessed with expectations: so much so that, for some, expectations are the only yardstick of economic success. They absolutely are not. Expectations, as we have discovered, are typically lagging indicators, adjusting only slowly to inflationary disturbances. A better way of characterising people's behaviour is via heuristics – or, more simply, rules of thumb. How these rules are formed, and how they adjust, is one of the big macroeconomic puzzles; yet ignoring them is a major error: after all, they help determine whether inflation is likely to remain low, whether it might end up a lot higher, and whether the central bank retains the public's trust.

Lesson 13: Policymakers are not easily able to distinguish inflationary squalls from periods of inflationary persistence

Understanding an inflationary evolution in real time is difficult. Some squalls remain squalls, while others develop into something far worse. It is, however, a mistake to assume that all squalls remain squalls. Central banks lack time machines to tell them what will happen in the future: they should neither assume they know what the future holds nor believe in their own lasting 'credibility' when faced with an initial inflationary surprise.

Lesson 14: All central banks should use the 'four tests' to judge whether, on balance, inflation is in danger of becoming a persistent problem

Given the absence of a workable time machine, a better way of assessing inflationary risk is to consider four tests, specifically: (i) have there been any institutional changes suggesting an increased bias in favour of inflation?; (ii) have there been signs of monetary excess sufficient to indicate a heightened inflationary risk?; (iii) is there evidence to suggest that a rising inflationary risk is being trivialised, notably through 'time machine' or 'external shock' arguments?; and (iv) have supply-side conditions changed for the worse?

Burton–Taylor revisited: getting the monetary–fiscal–financial mix right

Given our fourteen lessons, it's now time to think about what the future holds. It's not enough simply to hope for fewer pandemics or energy price shocks: the key drivers of inflation, as I have repeatedly emphasised, are not random accidents. They are, instead, weaknesses in both our ideas and our institutions, typically revealed when under maximum stress. Both our ideas and our institutions need to be improved.

Recall earlier arguments regarding the multiple objectives of central banks and the potential for those objectives to conflict with each other. In the absence of coordination between monetary and fiscal policy, these conflicts can be made a great deal worse.

Truss?

In September 2022, a new British prime minister and her chancellor decided to carry out an experiment. Fed up with an absence of decent UK economic growth, they announced a growth 'target' of 2.5 per cent – compared with an average annual growth rate of a little over 1 per cent in the recent past – to go alongside the existing 2 per cent inflation target. To achieve the growth target, Liz Truss and Kwasi Kwarteng announced a series of tax cuts (some of which were reversed only a few days later, as political and financial market support for Kwarteng's package rapidly evaporated). Described by Truss, Kwarteng and their cabal of supporters as policies designed to improve the 'supply-side' performance of the UK economy, the tax cuts looked suspiciously like old-fashioned 'demand-stimulus' policies. They were being adopted even as the UK economy was suffering an excess of inflation – mainly a reflection of the huge increase in energy prices stemming, at least in part, from the reduction in Russian gas supplies to Europe. Launched just after Kwarteng had sacked Tom Scholar, the most senior civil servant at the Treasury, and without the usual scrutiny offered by the independent Office for Budget Responsibility, the tax-cutting package went down badly in financial markets. With a lack of clarity regarding the impact of the tax cuts on government borrowing, gilt yields rose rapidly, triggering a series of 'liquidity shortages' and 'collateral calls' within pension funds that led to even more gilt sales and, thus, even higher yields: fiscal risks rapidly became financial risks.

These developments placed the Bank of England in a tricky position. On the one hand, its chief economist, Huw Pill, warned that the impact on the economy of the fiscal stimulus measures would likely require the bank to raise its policy rate by more than would otherwise have been the case. On the other hand, the sudden rise in gilt yields forced the bank to intervene in the gilt market the very next day, offering to buy £65 billion of government paper in a bid to drive yields back down and prevent a pension fund 'doom loop' from developing. Put another way, the bank apparently had to both *raise* interest rates in a bid to secure price stability and *cut* rates in a bid to prevent financial instability.

How had this happened? Two reasons stand out. The first – one that appears throughout this book – was the impact of quantitative easing. If governments know it's a tool lurking in the background, they also know it can always be used in the event of a financial emergency. Its presence creates a moral-hazard difficulty at the very heart of policymaking, encouraging governments to opt for financially risky policies in the knowledge that a central bank 'bailout' is always available. Whatever its occasional benefits during deflationary emergencies, it would be useful if quantitative easing could now be jettisoned: it has tilted the Burton–Taylor relationship in such a way that fiscal dominance has reappeared by the back door, in turn triggering financial fragilities.[2]

The second reason is a straightforward denial of the existence of the Burton–Taylor problem. Those supporting Truss simply ignored the problem, with one prominent economist claiming that 'monetary policy needs to curb inflation, fiscal policy to stabilise the economy'.[3] As I have repeatedly argued, however, such a separation of policy instruments doesn't work – either because it creates a 'pushmi-pullyu' confusion or, over the longer term, the separation leads to fiscal dominance, undermining the ability of an independent central bank to meet its inflation objectives.

Other than allowing fiscal watchdogs to perform the task they're supposed to perform (in other words, judging the sustainability or otherwise of fiscal policy under broadly plausible assumptions regarding the economy's future path), the best way of dealing with Burton–Taylor is to ensure that monetary policy enjoys primacy over fiscal policy. That means, first, that the central bank should be expected to comment on, and act upon, the monetary implications of any fiscal decision that changes longer-term borrowing plans; and second, that the central bank's mandate should ideally be restricted to price stability alone.[4]

Financial stability responsibilities should be housed elsewhere, thereby reducing the chances of the fiscal authority going down a path that forces the monetary authority to act against its best instincts or in an inconsistent manner. While this may create coordination issues – as indeed occurred during the Global Financial Crisis – it would remove the perception that a central bank exists primarily to bail out spendthrift governments in times of need. Politicians would thus be obliged to consider more carefully the monetary and financial consequences of their occasionally risky fiscal schemes.

It won't be easy. In a survey conducted on behalf of the European Central Bank to assess public perceptions of the Frankfurt-based behemoth, the control of inflation came only fifth on the list of the ECB's perceived objectives: tasks more widely recognised included financial stability, supporting those countries in financial difficulty, stabilising the euro and setting the level of interest rates. The aggregate numbers, meanwhile, disguised a huge variation in perception from country to country: 'keeping inflation at bay' was most likely to be mentioned by respondents in Finland (78 per cent), Germany (75 per cent) and Austria (74 per cent), but least likely to be cited by respondents in Latvia (23 per cent), Malta (33 per cent) and Greece (40 per cent).[5] A single currency area, it seems, can have multiple priorities, at least as far as its citizens are concerned. There may be huge variation in citizens' expectations of precisely what the ECB would do in the event of an inflationary shock that simultaneously threatened financial upheaval. It's not the sort of thing that encourages 'rules-based' clarity.

Through 2022, inflation across the eurozone rose to eye-wateringly high rates. Towards the end of that year, consumer prices were rising at a double-digit pace. The average, however, masked a range of experiences. In September, for example, French inflation, kept under control thanks to copious energy subsidies, was a mere 6.2 per cent. German inflation stood at a remarkable 10.9 per cent, probably the highest in the entire post-war period, and higher than Italy's 9.5 per cent. Dutch inflation had risen to a little over 17 per cent, while rates across the Baltic states were comfortably above 20 per cent. Policy rates, meanwhile, remained extraordinarily low.

As I argued in chapter 3, rising inflation rates were a reflection both of much higher gas prices and of the quasi-fiscal measures adopted by the European Central Bank. Fearing a widening of interest-rate spreads in the event of an aggressive monetary tightening, the ECB made the euro's survival a more important policy objective than price stability, promising to buy the bonds of any country that showed signs of a disorderly market, while acting only very slowly in response to rising price pressures. It was, in effect, a gamble. If energy prices subsequently collapse, following a resolution to the war in Ukraine, the gamble will have paid off. If, however, energy price increases stick, prompting price and wage increases elsewhere, the gamble will have failed.

Such a failure could, however, be on the most monumental of scales. To date, euro crises have mostly been about the so-called 'weak' members of the single currency – those faced with large current account deficits, rapidly rising borrowing costs and fears of either default or exit from the single currency. The future, however, may be rather different. Rapidly rising inflation in Germany and other northern European countries has so far been tolerated as a price worth paying for the preservation of the euro's integrity. Yet this requires Germany and its northern neighbours to accept economic conditions that, at any other time in their post-war history, would have been deemed totally unacceptable. Remember, the 1973 oil price shock led to hugely varying inflation outcomes across Europe, reflecting different attitudes towards price stability. If those attitudes resurface, the eurozone might eventually come unstuck – not through the financial eviction from the euro of its southern nations, but rather through the political rejection of the euro by its northern nations. It would be the post-American Civil War process in reverse.

Central bank independence in a world of high inflation

Given that people cannot always agree on the goals a central bank should be prioritising, politicians may not be content – or indeed able – to give central banks the specific inflation-busting powers that, for example, the Bundesbank enjoyed in the 1970s and 1980s. One justification for limiting central bank powers comes directly from the earlier chapters on the fairness or otherwise of both inflation and its eventual removal. Most central banks in the developed world (less so, perhaps, in the emerging world) have enjoyed a relatively easy ride in recent decades: they were often granted their independence when inflation was already low and they operated monetary policy during a period when inflation was, for the most part, well behaved. Put another way, few central bankers have been tested in circumstances where the job in hand is to push inflation down from an undesirably high level and when the political consequences of such actions are likely to be sizeable.

Admittedly, the reduction of inflation can be made easier when institutional reforms that enhance the credibility of the monetary and fiscal authorities are forthcoming. The biggest such reforms, however, are mostly one-offs. A central bank, for example, can only be granted its independence once: if, thereafter, it fails to deliver price stability, it is hardly surprising that it then comes under greater political scrutiny.

Indeed, arguably one reason why many central bankers have been so keen to insist that the rise in inflation during the pandemic and following the Ukraine war was temporary – and thus had nothing to do with their own policies – was the fear of admitting error. To do so might lead to difficult questions being asked in the corridors of power. An alternative strategy was to wait and hope that inflation would fade of its own accord.

Instead, inflation headed higher. As it did so, central banks found themselves in the firing line, targeted not just by politicians, but also, in some cases, by the general public. Since November 1999, the Bank of England has commissioned a quarterly survey of public attitudes to inflation, which asks, among other questions: 'Overall, how satisfied or dissatisfied are you with the way the Bank of England is doing its job to set interest rates in order to control inflation?'[6] Early in the survey's life, the public was remarkably supportive, with the net balance satisfied with the bank's performance sometimes above 60 per cent. Later, there were occasional dips, most obviously during and in the immediate aftermath of the Global Financial Crisis. At no point, however, did the net balance turn negative.

That all changed in 2022, when, thanks to what became known as the 'cost of living crisis', the public increasingly lost faith in the bank's inflation-fighting skills: at the time of writing, the balance is -7 per cent.

One way to think about the challenge facing independent central banks in a world of high inflation is to consider how they might have fared in the early 1980s, a time when inflation's defeat was far from guaranteed. Four examples are worth considering: (i) the Bundesbank; (ii) the Federal Reserve; (iii) the Banque de France; and (iv) the Bank of England.

The Bundesbank: a paragon of public trust

For the Bundesbank, life at the time was relatively easy. As an institution, it enjoyed the full support of a German population scarred by the folk memory of hyperinflation sixty years earlier. Successive governments knew better than to pick a fight with a central bank that, in the eyes of most Germans, was to be trusted far more than the average 'here today, gone tomorrow' politician.

The Fed: Volcker's gamble

The Federal Reserve's situation was slightly more complicated. Under Arthur F. Burns, who became its chairman in 1970, the Fed was partially responsible for the rapid increase in inflation in the 1970s: for much of that time, Burns himself simply refused to believe that the US central bank was in any way responsible for the unfolding mess.[7] Paul Volcker, appointed by President Carter in 1979, was tasked with sorting out the problem. He was helped by two factors: (i) although fiscal policy later headed in the 'wrong direction' from a Burton–Taylor perspective – with a huge amount of 'trickle-down' fiscal stimulus on offer – Volcker was able to raise 'real' interest rates into hugely positive territory, an outcome not matched by any of the major central banks in the post-pandemic era;[8] and (ii) as noted in chapter 5, high 'real' interest rates, and with them a rapidly ascending US dollar, imposed huge economic costs on those nations that had linked their monetary policies to those of the Federal Reserve: in time, as they succumbed to debt crises of one sort or another, the Fed in effect created a situation whereby the US was able to import disinflationary pressures from collapsing economies elsewhere in the world. Life as a central banker is a lot easier if you happen to be in control of the world's reserve currency.

An independent Banque de France during the Mitterrand growth experiment

Had an independent Banque de France existed in the early 1980s, it's difficult to believe that it would have been given as much leeway as the Bundesbank and the Federal Reserve. This, after all, was the time of the Mitterrand Experiment – an attempt to escape from economic orthodoxy via wholesale nationalisation, generous social benefits and huge tax increases for the wealthy. To keep inflation under control, the Banque de France would have had to deliver Volcker-style interest rates, doubtless leading to denunciation for undermining Mitterrand's experiment.

As it was, the markets did the work that the central bank would never have been able to do: the franc was devalued on multiple occasions within the confines of the Exchange Rate Mechanism of the European Monetary System, dropping against the Deutsche Mark from around 2.30 francs in 1980 to around 3.07 francs three years later. Eventually, a combination of excessive inflation, relentlessly rising unemployment and exchange-rate weakness forced Mitterrand to reverse course.[9]

The Bank of England as an independent 'Thatcherite' entity

As for the Bank of England, it is highly debatable whether, alone, it might have delivered the policies that ultimately led to a sustained reduction in inflation in the early 1980s. Those policies, after all, were enormously costly, with huge swathes of manufacturing industry wiped out, leading to a doubling of those unemployed. Matters were not helped by the fact that sterling rocketed in value on the foreign exchange markets.[10] Yet while Margaret Thatcher remains one of the most divisive British politicians of the post-war period, she at least had a democratic defence for her policies: she was re-elected in 1983 and again in 1987, suggesting that the country as a whole was prepared to swallow the bitter economic medicine. An independent central bank would surely have struggled to claim such democratic legitimacy.

These varying experiences in the early 1980s suggest that the debate regarding the independence or otherwise of central banks is not as straightforward as it might at first appear. While central bank independence can immunise monetary policy against political timetables, the really tough policy decisions – most obviously the costs associated with squeezing excessive inflation out of the system – may ultimately require some form of political validation. In Germany's case, that validation was provided by a collective folk memory. In the UK's case, the validation was surely provided only by successive election victories and a lingering memory among the public of the inflationary chaos of the 1970s.

Put simply, the bigger the inflationary challenge, the more politicised the answer is likely to be, and thus the greater the requirement for some form of political intervention. From the late 1980s through to the immediate pre-pandemic world, central banks mostly managed to avoid this problem: inflation was low and stable, and most of the criticism aimed at central banks focused on issues of financial stability, notably around the time of the Global Financial Crisis. The post-pandemic inflationary surge made life for central bankers a lot more complicated: taking tough action when politicians were all promising to 'build back better' was not exactly easy, but avoiding tough action may have contributed to a further acceleration in inflationary pressures. Escaping from the political spotlight in these circumstances is, to say the least, tricky.

Further institutional reforms: tackling groupthink

Towards the end of 2022, inflation seemed to be everywhere. No longer did it appear to be a transitory squall. For central banks, this was a major surprise. As late as December 2021, the Federal Reserve was saying that 'progress on vaccinations and an easing of supply constraints are expected to support continued gains in economic activity and employment as well as a reduction in inflation'.[11] Three months earlier, even though UK inflation was already at 3.2 per cent and the Bank of England was warning of a possible breach of 4 per cent early the following year, the view was nevertheless that 'current elevated cost pressures would prove transitory. Indeed, there were still good reasons to expect material supply responses in commodity and other global markets, pushing down on future input prices and import costs.' To be fair, the bank added that 'current elevated inflationary pressures could potentially lead to some second-round effect on consumer prices', but it never-theless concluded that 'UK inflation expectations remain well anchored'.[12]

What is striking about these two episodes is not the central statements offered by the two central banks, in both cases broadly dismissive of any lasting inflationary threat. Rather, there was very little, if any, dissent. The Federal Open Market Committee unanimously endorsed the December statement. The Bank of England's Monetary Policy Committee (MPC) mostly agreed on the September statement.[13] Given what had already happened with money supply growth, with the spread of inflation through to the broader economy, with labour market developments and, little by little, with inflationary expectations, the level of agreement was remarkable. It was almost as if the two committees had fallen for their own prop-aganda, confident in the belief that their policies would always be regarded as credible.

It wasn't always so. Under Paul Volcker in the 1980s and in Alan Greenspan's early years as Volcker's successor, dissent was common on the Federal Open Market Committee, with dissenters sometimes offering completely opposing views: some would argue in favour of larger interest-rate increases, while others advocated smaller increases or possibly even cuts.[14] Similar divergences of opinion occurred on the MPC. In 2008, the year of the Global Financial Crisis, one member of the committee voted for rate cuts, while another favoured rate increases. They both had their reasons, even if, in hindsight, one option appears to have been more forward looking than the other.[15]

The key conclusion, however, is that uncertainty is better reflected in a lack of consensus. There will be occasions when the incoming information will carry ambiguous implications for the future. That ambiguity, in turn, should be visible in the amount of dissent shown within a committee's decision-making process. Put differently, an absence of dissent shows that the committee is not doing its job properly. This is particularly so during periods when an economy is subject to considerable shocks.

Yet, after Volcker and Alan Greenspan's early years, such dissent slowly faded from view. The respective monetary committees eventually began to demonstrate what appeared to be 'groupthink'. Such behaviour raises serious questions about the composition of the committees. Does it make sense, for example, for all four deputy governors of the Bank of England to have worked previously at HM Treasury? Is it appropriate that the four external members of the Monetary Policy Committee should be appointed through an interview process that is run entirely by HM Treasury, with the same former 'external member' of the MPC on the selection panel on every single occasion since 2011? Is it right that one of the deputy governors should have run the recruitment process for external members under his previous role at the Treasury? Should an external member of the committee – brought in, presumably, for his independence of thought – then be appointed a deputy governor? What incentive does such an appointment offer other external members to question the 'received wisdom' of the institution?

Then there's the thorny issue of committee chairmanship. Is the chair willing to tolerate dissent? Someone with a narcissistic personality, for example, might be charm personified if the other committee members agree with him (or her), but might equally be hostile – in the form of angry outbursts and cold shouldering – if challenged. Such behaviour, in turn, might encourage those others meekly to toe the line: most people would rather have an easy life than deal with persistent conflict. Meanwhile, some policies only 'work' if dissent is banished: forward guidance, which projects a path for the future level of policy rates based on a monetary committee's best assessment of what lies ahead economically, is only likely to be credible if there is broad agreement about what, roughly, the future will be. Yet while there may be rare situations in which such unanimity is necessary – notably when a central bank promises to be 'irresponsible' in a bid to raise expectations of future inflation, thus lowering current 'real' interest rates at the zero-rate bound – these must be regarded as the exception to the general rule. Normalising such moments of unanimity simply turns the supposedly credible into the foolishly implausible.[16]

Admittedly, it's not possible to make dissent a requirement of committee work: there will be occasions when unanimity is entirely appropriate. Still, dissent – as captured by differing policy votes – should be regarded as a sign of successful and healthy committee behaviour in a world of economic and financial uncertainty. By implication, an extended absence of dissent should be seen as a sign of potential failure. Those to whom central banks are accountable – congressional committees, parliamentary committees, the media – should encourage such dissent: it is more likely to indicate the presence of constructive debate about the appropriate monetary policy than is the alternative of possibly complacent unanimity.

Put another way, central bank independence on its own provides no real guarantee of policy success. The dynamics of the decision-making committee are also important: not paying attention to those dynamics may lead to bad policy decisions, irrespective of the broader economic and political environment.

One-way bets and financial instability

Monetary policy has financial consequences. And monetary policy as a one-way bet has extreme financial consequences. Episodes that immediately spring to mind are: (i) the dot-com bubble (fuelled by Alan Greenspan's short-lived belief in a late-1990s 'high growth, low inflation' new paradigm), an asset price boom that eventually popped, ushering in a modest recession and thereafter a slump in productivity growth; (ii) the pre-Global Financial Crisis 'hunt for yield', a period during which declining long-term interest rates, partly a reflection of the global savings glut, helped fuel the sub-prime boom; and (iii) Japan's late-1980s asset price boom, fuelled by the so-called 'triple merits' of low oil prices, a rising yen and persistently low inflation.

In all three cases, hopes that policy rates could be permanently lower were eventually undermined by the re-emergence of inflation. With policy rates forced higher, and growth expectations thus forced lower, asset markets tumbled: the one-way bets that had led the Nikkei 225, the NASDAQ and the US housing market to boom unravelled at a rate of knots. As optimism fell and the liquidity tide went out, so financial weaknesses were exposed: in Japan, banks proved brutally vulnerable to cross-shareholdings and property exposures, while in the US, the sub-prime crisis revealed 'off balance sheet' bets which crippled the entire financial system.

Post-pandemic, the rise in inflation was far greater. The need for monetary restraint might, in time, prove significant. Such restraint, however, would carry substantial financial stability risks. The entire period since the Global Financial Crisis surely qualifies as a prime example of a 'one-way bet' on nominal interest rates: we were, after all, supposedly in a world of disinflation or deflation rather than inflation, and so interest rates were apparently to remain at rock bottom. Such views were reinforced both by the persistence of quantitative easing and by regulations requiring banks and others to hold more in the way of 'safe' government bonds to shore up their capital ratios in the aftermath of the Global Financial Crisis.

At the time of writing, many of these 'one-way bets' are in danger of becoming 'two-way bets'. In September 2022, weaknesses in UK pension funds were exposed, as gilt yields rose, triggering collateral demands that led to more in the way of forced selling. Housing markets the world over boomed during and after the pandemic, supported by the perception that interest rates could never rise. As bond yields spiked, the risk of major housing market corrections escalated. Cryptocurrencies – possibly the most obvious speculative beneficiary of persistently easy money – suddenly looked enormously vulnerable. Meanwhile, those governments unable politically to control their fiscal incontinence – perhaps because they find themselves having to offer bailouts to an increasing number of needy sectors of the economy – might, in time, trigger further, country-specific bond yield increases, alongside sudden and rapid currency corrections.

The danger is obvious. If the one-way bets turn out to be as big as they have been in the past, while fiscal positions are far weaker (thanks to huge increases in government debt) and inflationary threats are much greater, the risk of bad economic and financial outcomes has surely increased: if monetary policy has to be tightened, the need for fiscal-led bailouts may increase in circumstances where fiscal policy is poorly placed to act. One way of coping – hardly ideal – is simply not to bother fighting inflation and blame its presence on unforeseen external shocks and the reversal of globalisation trends, over which no individual country has any real influence. As the Bank for International Settlements pointedly remarks, however, while higher inflation

> helped limit the rise in [government] debt-to-GDP ratios ... surprise inflation is not a mechanism that fiscal or monetary authorities can or should rely on to control public debt over the medium term ... The large stocks of government debt held by central banks complicate matters ... In effect, they transform long-term fixed income into debt indexed at the overnight rate ... The general picture brings into sharp focus the tensions between fiscal and monetary policy along the normalisation path. These could heighten the pressure on central banks to keep their stance more accommodative than appropriate.[17]

Inflation is never dead. Sometimes it (badly) offers a way out for policymakers who feel that all the other alternatives are even worse.

Inflation protection

This is a book about the causes and consequences of inflation, not a series of recommendations regarding asset allocation. There are plenty of books offering such advice. Most, however, suffer from a rather obvious problem. Knowing whether we're at the beginning of an inflationary period, or rather at the start of a sustained attempt to rid ourselves of inflation, is tricky, to say the least. In hindsight, however, the call on inflation is one of the most important drivers of asset allocation. At 5.6 per cent, inflation was high in 1970, when Arthur Burns took over the reins at the Federal Reserve. It was both higher and rising rapidly when he left office. Given the risks involved, 1970 would not have been a good year in which to invest in equities: in four of the following eight years, real equity returns were negative – as indeed they were across the eight years as a whole. Over the entirety of Burns's time in office, investors in equities and bonds lost roughly equal amounts in real terms. There were modest gains to be had from investing in corporate bonds or real estate; but for the most part, financial markets emerged from this period bruised and battered.

By contrast, 1979 was an excellent year in which to invest in equities: during the Volcker era – a period during which inflation initially tumbled – the average equity investor doubled her money in real terms. Returns on bonds were also excellent: the Treasury market yielded a real return of 60 per cent over Volcker's eight years, while corporate bonds delivered 94 per cent. One 'asset', however, did much worse: the price of gold rose more than fivefold between 1970 and 1978, but by only 30 per cent between 1979 and 1987. Indeed, the latter period contained two distinct stories: substantial further gains between 1979 and 1980, as investors questioned Volcker's resolve, followed by sustained losses. Put simply, while an absence of inflation credibility leads to huge demand for precious metal, the return of such credibility may lead to an equally huge reversal in demand.[18]

The Burns and Volcker experiences suggest, however, that investors need to think very carefully about the political economy of inflation. Is inflation politically preferable to a series of grim fiscal alternatives? Have the authorities recognised the inflation threat, or has it been conveniently swept under the carpet? Does fiscal dominance threaten central bank independence? Are financial stability risks so great that inflation cannot be properly dealt with? Will a policy-induced recession lead to the removal of inflation, or rather will it lead to premature monetary easing, allowing inflation to ratchet higher from one economic cycle to the next?

Without answers, investors are left with the tricky challenge of managing uncertainty and, alongside it, potentially huge volatility. After all, periods of great uncertainty in financial markets can also be associated with major shifts in conviction from one year to the next. The winning bet in one year could thus turn into the losing bet the following year, as happened during the 1970s. Under these difficult circumstances, the only real option is diversification.

The years of low inflation reduced diversification opportunities hugely: with most countries facing similarly limited price pressures and well-behaved bond markets, the benefits of diversification were modest, if indeed such diversification opportunities even existed. The return of inflation – and the associated threat of financial instability – has changed all that. A few simple maxims should help:

- Don't invest in only one country or currency area, because you might choose the one that is less able than others to control inflation, thereby increasing currency risk.[19]
- Don't assume, as investors often do, that equities offer tremendous inflation protection: they didn't in the inflationary 1970s.
- Do have some exposure to gold, just in case we really are at one of those historic moments when inflation persists over an indefinite period of time.
- Accept that cash and bank deposits will deliver negative returns, and therefore excessive caution will be penalised.
- Given the negative real yields, think carefully about whether you could be the next Hugo Stinnes, leveraging yourself up

to acquire real assets (few will find themselves in such a fortunate position).

- And maybe take a 'sleeper' bet on the future of the euro, based on a reversal of the evidence accumulated after the American Civil War: any hint of inflation-inspired political ructions at the heart of the eurozone would turn northern European bond markets into high-returning 'quasi currencies'.

And finally . . .

Both Arthur Burns and Paul Volcker delivered Per Jacobsson lectures shortly after their departure from the Federal Reserve.[20] History judges Burns to have failed on inflation. Volcker, though, is regarded as an all-conquering hero who vanquished inflation. At first glance, it's an unfair conclusion: under Burns, US inflation averaged 6.5 per cent per annum, while under Volcker, it averaged 5.4 per cent – only a little lower. However, when Burns left office, inflation was 6.8 per cent and rising rapidly; when Volcker departed, it stood at only 4.3 per cent – and earlier in his tenure, it had been even lower.

Burns's 1979 speech revealed grave doubts about the inflation-busting opportunities available to central bankers. At the time, inflation remained uncomfortably high. Burns asked some key questions:

Why is the worldwide disease of inflation proving so stubborn? Why is it not yielding to the various efforts of the affected nations, including some determined efforts, to bring it to an end? Why, in particular, have central bankers, whose main business one might suppose is to fight inflation, been so ineffective in dealing with this worldwide problem?

Dwelling on the third of these questions, Burns observed that:

> By training, if not also by temperament, [central bankers] are inclined to lay great stress on price stability, and their abhorrence of inflation is continually reinforced by contacts with one another and with like-minded members of the private financial community. And yet, despite their antipathy towards inflation and the powerful weapons they could wield against it, central bankers have failed so utterly in this mission in recent years. In this paradox lies the anguish of central banking.

Burns took a proto-Reaganite view in his explanation for inflationary tendencies in the US economy: the state was too big, expectations of continued economic progress were too great, social support programmes were too generous, etc., etc. His view was that these 'worldwide philosophic and political trends inevitably affected [central banks'] attitudes and actions'. As far as the Fed was concerned, it

> had the power to abort the inflation at its incipient stage fifteen years ago or at any later period, and it has the power to end it today ... it did not do so because the Federal Reserve was itself caught up in the philosophic and political currents that were transforming American life and culture.

In other words, there wasn't any appetite for imposing sufficiently distasteful monetary medicine, including significantly positive real interest rates. Had the Fed done so,

> severe difficulties could be quickly produced in the economy ... facing these political realities, the Federal Reserve was

still willing to step hard on the monetary brakes at times . . .
but its restrictive stance was not maintained long enough to
end inflation.

Fast forward now to 1990. Paul Volcker pondered on a key
shift in perceptions:

> What intrigues me is why the status of central banks is
> higher today than only a decade or so ago, the extent to
> which those institutions are really in better control of our
> financial destinies, and what all that implies for sustaining
> growth and stability.

His explanation was simple: as inflation proved to be an
increasingly stubborn adversary, so other aspects of economic
life – 'growth, employment, productivity' – slowly deteriorated.
'In those circumstances, the monetarist refrain that inflation
is, after all, in the end a monetary phenomenon struck an
increasing [*sic*] responsive chord among the body politic.' In
other words, as economic realities changed, so political possi-
bilities also began to shift.

To be fair, the medicine meted out by central banks was hardly
pleasant. 'One country after another was caught up in recession
or an extended period of stagnation. But, in the end, inflation did
recede. Then . . . expansion got under way.' Later in his speech,
Volcker offered some thoughts on the control of inflation more
generally: 'The best results [in delivering price stability] will be
achieved if the inflationary threat is dealt with at an early stage,
before the public is fully alarmed, and that procrastination only
invites greater difficulty.' Moreover, 'vacuous admonitions that a
monetary authority can be all things to all men – for growth, full
employment, and stability – risk confusion and misunderstanding

about what a central bank can really do'. And 'an attempt to validate imprudent lending practices by excessive monetary expansion, even if seemingly successful in the short run, would surely soon breed more excesses'.

Volcker, the man who more than anyone helped defeat inflation, died in 2019 at the age of 92. Many of the lessons he learnt through his professional life are in danger of being forgotten. Post-pandemic, inflation was not dealt with at an early stage. The public understandably became very alarmed. Under pressure from the political classes, central banks strove to be 'all things to all men'. And we became so terrified of financial instability that we began to forget how dangerous inflation could be.

Burns may have failed in his allotted task, but he understood that the evolution of inflation is very much a political process: independent or otherwise, central banks cannot operate in a vacuum. It may well be that central banks will, from time to time, step on the monetary brakes. Their resolve to do so in a world in which politicians promise to 'build back better', or to raise the trend growth rate, or to preserve the integrity of the single currency will now be tested as never before. Those who like to believe we still live in a Volcker-led world might need to prepare instead for a return to the crazy world of Arthur Burns.

Notes

Preface

1. Most obviously, bond yields began to rise rapidly, if belatedly, in response to renewed signs of inflation, while Liz Truss and Kwasi Kwarteng got into terrible trouble in the UK after their 'unbudgeted' fiscal plans announced in September 2022 threatened both higher inflation and weaker sterling: gilt yields rose abruptly as a result.
2. See S.D. King, *Grave New World: The end of globalization, the return of history*, revised edition, Yale University Press, London, 2018.
3. The IMF's June 2020 World Economic Outlook Update offered the following – typical – take on inflationary risks: 'Inflation projections have generally been revised downward, with larger cuts typically in 2020 and for advanced economies. This generally reflects a combination of weaker activity and lower commodity prices, although in some cases partially offset by the effect of exchange-rate depreciation on import prices. Inflation is expected to rise gradually in 2021, consistent with the projected pickup in activity. Nonetheless, the inflation outlook remains muted, reflecting expectations of persistently weak aggregate demand.' The link to the full report is available at https://www.imf.org/en/Publications/WEO/Issues/2020/06/24/WEOUpdateJune2020. In April 2021, the IMF predicted 'Inflation Pressure to Remain Contained in Most Countries'.
4. See S. King, 'Despite what central bankers say we're right to worry about inflation', *Evening Standard*, May 2021, available at https://www.

standard.co.uk/comment/comment/despite-central-bankers-right-to-worry-inflation-b935602.html

5. See, for example, L. Summers, 'The inflation risk is real', May 2021, available at http://larrysummers.com/2021/05/24/the-inflation-risk-is-real/ or C. Rugaber, 'Inflation ahead? Even a top economist says it's complicated', AP News, June 2021, available at https://apnews.com/article/lifestyle-inflation-business-536d99a7a2d7abf8dd735963e57b237f, quoting Furman.

6. M. Wolf, 'The return of the inflation spectre', *Financial Times*, 26 March 2021, available at https://www.ft.com/content/6cfb36ca-d3ce-4dd3-b70d-eecc332ba1df; 'As inflation rises, the monetarist dog is having its day', *Financial Times*, 22 February 2022, available at https://www.ft.com/content/0cd1d666-8842-4c82-8344-07c4e433a408; 'Inflation is a political challenge as well as an economic one', *Financial Times*, 12 July 2022, available at https://www.ft.com/content/2022df1d-57c5-44a4-93e6-73f5f5274ca8 (subscription required).

7. R. Cookson, 'Brace yourself for a sharp rise in inflation', Bloomberg, November 2020, available at https://finance.yahoo.com/news/inflation-may-pick-sharply-060002710.html

8. C. Goodhart and M. Pradhan, *The Great Demographic Reversal: Ageing societies, waning inequality and an inflation revival*, Palgrave Macmillan/Springer Nature, Cham (Switzerland), 2020.

Chapter 1: The resurrection of inflation

1. See, for example, R. Bootle, *The Death of Inflation: Surviving and thriving in the zero era*, Nicholas Brealey Publishing, London, 1996.

2. Japan's 'stagnation' is not quite so stagnant when we look at income per head of the working-age population: population ageing, not deflation, has been the biggest contributor to perceived economic weakness.

3. Turkish inflation averaged 76 per cent per annum in the 1990s. Source: IMF World Economic Outlook database, April 2022.

4. See, for example, https://www.thisismoney.co.uk/money/news/article-3240112/Research-shows-Mars-Bars-shrunk-28-1990s-Yorkies-20-1980s.html

5. A. Smith, *The Wealth of Nations*, ed. A. Skinner, Penguin, London, 1982.

6. See K. Arrow and G. Debreu, 'Existence of an equilibrium for a competitive economy', *Econometrica*, 22:3 (1954).

7. For a more detailed discussion, see, for example, https://www.ons.gov.uk/economy/inflationandpriceindices/articles/coronaviruscovid19andconsumerpriceinflationweightsandprices/2021

8. See https://www.cambridge.org/core/books/abs/collected-writings-of-john-maynard-keynes/inflation-1919/840D10594658FB428E59B97CA1EB3AE5

9. E. de Waal, *The Hare with Amber Eyes: A hidden inheritance*, Vintage, London, 2011.

10. See, for example, 'Argentina's new, honest inflation statistics: The end of bogus accounting', *The Economist*, 25 May 2017, available at https://www.economist.com/the-americas/2017/05/25/argentinas-new-honest-inflation-statistics
11. B. Bernanke, 'The Great Moderation: Remarks at the meetings of the Eastern Economic Association', February 2004, available at https://www.federalreserve.gov/boarddocs/speeches/2004/20040220/
12. 'Probably', because there is no consistent series that reliably splices West Germany pre-reunification with Germany post-reunification.
13. Quantitative easing covers a multitude of asset purchase schemes, but in all cases the aim is to buy financial assets in a bid to change relative prices and yields in ways that will encourage companies to raise funds and households to spend more.
14. ibid.
15. I. Schnabel, 'The globalisation of inflation', address to a conference organised by the Österreichische Vereinigung für Finanzanalyse und Asset Management, available at https://www.ecb.europa.eu/press/key/date/2022/html/ecb.sp220511_1~e9ba02e127.en.html
16. F. Panetta, 'Normalising monetary policy in non-normal times', policy lecture hosted by the SAFE Policy Center at Goethe University and the Centre for Economic Policy Research, available at https://www.ecb.europa.eu/press/key/date/2022/html/ecb.sp220525~eef274e856.en.html
17. W. Brainard, 'Uncertainty and the effectiveness of policy', *American Economic Review*, 57:2 (1967), Papers and Proceedings of the Seventy-ninth Annual Meeting of the American Economic Association.
18. Pangloss was Candide's mentor in the eponymous novel by Voltaire. His character was a thinly veiled attack on the optimism of Leibniz and his followers.

Chapter 2: A history of inflation, money and ideas

1. See D. Paarlberg, *An Analysis and History of Inflation*, Praeger, Westport, CT, 1993.
2. To be fair, such an increase didn't work out at a huge amount on an annual basis. An average 3.6 per cent annual increase in the price level was enough, cumulatively, to lead to huge long-term monetary destruction. Yet that cumulative effect was felt by some far more than others. Even two thousand years ago, inflation created both winners and losers.
3. Mercury was a vital ingredient in the production of silver. Thanks to cinnabar smelting, huge volumes of mercury vapour were released into the environment – poisoning flora, fauna and humans in the process – during the colonial period. See, for example, N. Robins and N. Hagan, 'Mercury production and use in colonial Andean silver production: Emissions and health implications', *Environmental Health Perspectives*, 120:5 (2012).

4. This section draws on O. Volckart, 'Early beginnings of the quantity theory of money and their context in Polish and Prussian monetary policies, c.1520–1550', *Economic History Review*, New Series, 50:3 (1997).

5. In the 1970s, when for a while the copper in UK coins was worth more than their face value, some proposed that London Transport should melt down the many thousands of accumulated lost coins to cover some of its costs. It would probably have been illegal.

6. The modern-day Polish *złoty* is a direct translation into Polish of *gulden*, the historic German and Dutch term for a gold coin.

7. See T. Levenson, *Money for Nothing: The South Sea Bubble and the invention of modern capitalism*, Random House, New York, 2020.

8. Locke's arguments are similar to the 'King Canute' theory espoused by Mervyn King more than three centuries later. For a summary, see https://www.theguardian.com/business/2021/nov/23/central-banks-have-king-canute-theory-of-inflation-says-former-governor

9. I. Fisher, assisted by H.G. Brown, *The Purchasing Power of Money: Its determination and relation to credit, interest and crisis*, Macmillan, New York, 1911.

10. For a more detailed discussion of these issues, see, for example, T.M. Humphrey, 'The quantity theory of money: Its historical evolution and role in policy debates', *Federal Reserve of Richmond Economic Review*, May/June 1974, available at https://core.ac.uk/download/pdf/6917453.pdf

11. See J. Goldstone, 'Monetary versus velocity interpretations of the "price revolution": A comment', *Journal of Economic History*, 51:1 (1991), pp. 176–181.

12. In 2010, a number of eminent economists and others wrote an open letter – published by the *Wall Street Journal* – to Ben Bernanke, then chairman of the Federal Reserve. They advocated the immediate discontinuation of quantitative easing, arguing that 'the planned asset purchases risk currency debasement and inflation'. In some cases, their misjudged warnings proved to be no impediment to subsequent career advancement. Following President Trump's nomination, David Malpass, one of the signatories, was later appointed president of the World Bank. See https://www.wsj.com/articles/BL-REB-12460 (subscription required).

13. Keynes also worried about his 'liquidity trap', a situation in which increased money supply would only lead to more money held, rather than spent.

14. M. Friedman and A. Schwartz, *A Monetary History of the United States, 1867–1960*, National Bureau of Economic Research, Cambridge, MA, 1963.

15. In truth, the Friedman attack has been interpreted using three subtly different arguments: (i) money supply has no impact on real economic outcomes; (ii) money supply does have an effect, but the lags are long,

variable and not terribly predictable, and thus attempts to exploit the effect will only introduce unwanted volatility into an economy; and (iii) inflation can be caused by exogenous shocks, rather than excess monetary growth, but is only likely to persist if those shocks are 'accommodated' via inappropriate monetary expansion thereafter.

16. See C. Calomiris and J. Mason, 'Consequences of bank distress during the Great Depression', *American Economic Review*, 93:3 (2003).

17. 'Remarks by Governor Ben S. Bernanke at the conference to honor Milton Friedman', University of Chicago, Illinois, 8 November 2002, available at https://www.federalreserve.gov/boarddocs/speeches/2002/20021108/

18. One such example is S. Pamuk, 'Prices in the Ottoman Empire, 1469–1914', *International Journal of Middle East Studies*, 36 (2004). Like many other such authors, Pamuk had to rely on limited data, focused primarily on food. Sources included account books from a mixture of (i) pious foundations (*vakif*) and their soup kitchens (*imaret*); (ii) prices paid by the Topkapi palace kitchen; and (iii) officially established price ceilings (*narh*). Foods within the indices included flour, rice, animal fat, honey, mutton, chickpeas and olive oil. Non-food items included soap, wood, coal and nails (reflecting construction costs).

19. F.H. Capie (ed.), *Major Inflations in History*, Edward Elgar, Aldershot, 1991.

20. Another interesting example of how people think about money – as opposed to what the authorities do with it – comes from Iraq between the Gulf Wars. See M. King, *The End of Alchemy: Money, banking and the future of the global economy*, Little, Brown, London, 2016.

21. Being paid back 'in full' did not necessarily mean a return of capital: it might, instead, reflect a commitment to receiving from the government a perpetual stream of income.

22. To that extent, there is a clear similarity with the expansion of collateralised debt obligations in the years running up to the Global Financial Crisis, liquid AAA-rated pieces of paper that, in truth, were often backed by illiquid sub-prime mortgages of highly uncertain value. Like the *assignats*, they fell victim to a collapse in confidence.

23. R.L. Spang, *Stuff and Money in the Time of the French Revolution*, Harvard University Press, Cambridge, MA, 2015.

24. For a detailed discussion, see, for example, C.D. Campbell and G. Tullock, 'Hyperinflation in China, 1937–49', *Journal of Political Economy*, 62:3 (1954).

25. See J.M. Keynes, 'The economic consequences of Mr Churchill' (1925), in E. Johnson and D. Moggridge (eds), *The Collected Writings of John Maynard Keynes*, Vol. IX, *Essays in Persuasion*, Cambridge University Press for the Royal Economic Society, 1978.

26. See B. Bernanke and H. James, 'The gold standard, deflation, and financial crisis in the Great Depression: An international comparison' (1991), in B. Bernanke, *Essays on the Great Depression*, Princeton

University Press, Princeton, NJ, 2004 or B. Eichengreen, *Golden Fetters: The gold standard and the Great Depression 1919–1939* (NBER Series on Long-term Factors in Economic Development), Oxford University Press, New York/Oxford, 1992.

27. Edward I reigned from 1272 to 1307. Nicknamed 'Longshanks', at 6 feet 2 inches he was unusually tall for his time. He was also a bit of an antisemite, having issued the 'Edict of Expulsion' in 1290, leading to the expulsion of Jews from England. They weren't welcomed back until Oliver Cromwell took charge three and a half centuries later.

28. Some have argued that the persistent loss of monetary value in the UK in the twentieth century began specifically in 1936, the year in which John Maynard Keynes published his General Theory. Correlation, however, does not necessarily imply causation.

29. There are exceptions, most obviously the deflations witnessed in the 1930s and, much more recently, the very modest deflations seen in Japan and the eurozone.

Chapter 3: The inflationary role of governments

1. The US dollar came off the gold standard in 1933. A renewed link with gold was established with the formation of the Bretton Woods system of fixed but adjustable exchange rates in the immediate aftermath of the Second World War. The link was severed by President Nixon in 1971.

2. United States House of Representatives, 'The Legislation Placing "In God We Trust" on National Currency', Historical Highlights, History, Art & Archives, available at https://history.house.gov/Historical-Highlights/1951-2000/The-legislation-placing-%E2%80%9CIn-God-We-Trust%E2%80%9D-on-national-currency/

3. G.C. Eggleston, *A Rebel's Recollections* (1875), reprinted by Indiana University Press, Bloomington, IN, 1959.

4. Other things may also change. As with Brazil, a government using generous inflation indexation arrangements may not benefit quite so much from rising inflation: any wage or pension, for example, that is indexed will have to rise in line with inflation, negating the advantage the government finances might otherwise enjoy. More recent examples of this 'problem' include the UK's pension 'triple lock', in which pensions increase by the highest of earnings growth, price inflation or 2.5 per cent a year.

5. After Taylor's death in 2011, rumours abounded that, in accordance with her wishes, she would either be buried alongside her former husband in Geneva (where Burton's remains are) or they would be buried together in Pontrhydyfen, near Port Talbot (where Burtons have apparently been buried for many years). In the event, her body remained in Los Angeles, although she took to the grave his last, unpublished, love letter to her – written only a few days before he died.

6. See, for example, https://www.whitehouse.gov/about-the-white-house/presidents/franklin-d-roosevelt/

7. Other explanations included: in the UK, a desire to boost money supply by increasing the banks' deposits at the Bank of England; and in the US, a desire to force equity prices higher, in the hope of generating a wealth effect. In truth, no one knew for sure how the 'experiment' might play out.

8. Interestingly, as soon as quantitative-easing policies threatened to go into reverse against a background of clearly rising inflation, the vigilantes showed signs of returning: their actions, in part, brought the short-lived government of Liz Truss in the UK to a premature end.

9. See, for example, 'People's inflation expectations are rising – and will be hard to bring down', *The Economist*, June 2022, available at https://www.economist.com/finance-and-economics/2022/06/19/peoples-inflation-expectations-are-rising-and-will-be-hard-to-bring-down

10. For a useful discussion, see Office for Budget Responsibility, 'Debt maturity, quantitative easing and interest rate sensitivity', Economic and Fiscal Outlook, March 2021, available at https://obr.uk/box/debt-maturity-quantitative-easing-and-interest-rate-sensitivity/

11. The fiscal theory of the price level has relevance here, as argued in J.H. Cochrane, 'The fiscal theory of the price level' (2021), available at https://static1.squarespace.com/static/5e6033a4ea02d801f37e15bb/t/61b79f3e95fc6559bce8ed34/1639423807095/Fiscal_theory_JEP.pdf

12. Draghi made his famous speech on 23 July 2012.

13. See, for example, https://www.ecb.europa.eu/press/pr/date/2022/html/ecb.pr220721~973e6e7273.en.html

14. ibid.

15. See https://braveneweurope.com/dirk-ehnts-warren-mosler-a-euro-zone-proposal-for-fighting-the-economic-consequences-of-the-coronavirus-crisis

16. S. Kelton, *The Deficit Myth: Modern Monetary Theory and how to build a better economy*, John Murray, London, 2020.

17. ibid.

18. See https://braveneweurope.com/dirk-ehnts-warren-mosler-a-euro-zone-proposal-for-fighting-the-economic-consequences-of-the-coronavirus-crisis

19. A much-used alternative – or addition – is rationing.

20. A treaty not specified: oil prices collapsed in 1985, but the Iran–Iraq War continued until the 1988 stalemate; and in any case, inflationary experiences varied hugely, suggesting that differences in monetary policy were playing an important role.

21. S. Kelton, 'There are so many things we could be doing – together – to crush inflation', June 2022, available at https://stephaniekelton.substack.com/p/catch-me-on-the-mehdi-hasan-show

22. ibid.

23. J.M. Keynes, *How to Pay for the War: A radical plan for the chancellor of the Exchequer*, Macmillan and Co. Limited, London, 1940, available at https://fraser.stlouisfed.org/files/docs/historical/Misc/howtopayforthewar_1940.pdf

24. Inflation is also a mechanism to drag people into higher tax brackets if, for example, allowances are not increased in line with rising prices.

25. The idea was to avoid the temptations of the Siren voices, which lured sailors onto the rocky cliffs.

Chapter 4: The case for resisting inflationary temptations

1. See http://content.time.com/time/covers/0,16641,19230317,00.html

2. 'The Ruhr', *Time* magazine, 17 March 1923, available at https://content.time.com/time/subscriber/article/0,33009,715096,00.html

3. World Inequality Database, specifically https://wid.world/country/united-kingdom/

4. The irony is that, in 2021 and onwards, higher than expected inflation was blamed on departure from the EU.

5. See J.E. Alt, *The Politics of Economic Decline: Economic management and political behaviour in Britain since 1964*, Cambridge University Press, Cambridge, 1979; and J. Tomlinson, 'British government and popular understanding of inflation in the mid-1970s', *Economic History Review*, 67:3 (2014).

6. HMSO, 'Attack on Inflation: A Policy for Survival: A guide to the Government's Programme', Crown Copyright, August 1975, available at https://wdc.contentdm.oclc.org/digital/collection/tav/id/53

7. For the record, the equivalent West German numbers were 5.6 per cent and 3.6 per cent.

8. In 1976, two British academics observed – presciently – that 'there is a strong presumption that the declining exchange rate was in part related to the conduct of monetary policy'. See R.J. Ball and T. Burns, 'The inflationary mechanism in the UK economy', *American Economic Review*, 66:4 (1976). Burns – now The Lord Burns GCB – became the Treasury's chief economic adviser in 1980 and was directly associated with the Medium Term Financial Strategy, the hallmark financial framework adopted by Margaret Thatcher's Conservatives in the 1980s. In the mid-1970s, however, even he couldn't quite let go of incomes policies: in 'The inflationary mechanism', Ball and Burns conclude by observing that an incomes policy 'can help in preventing the community from attempting to price itself at a level that is inconsistent with the country's overall efficiency levels in relation to world markets and to prevent erosion of the necessary rate of profitability without the necessity of creating massive unemployment in order to achieve the same objective'. In the event, incomes policies were abandoned, and massive unemployment became a reality.

9. Different rules apply to telephone waiting times: unlike the supermarket experience, it is more difficult to see how many 'people' are in

front of you and how many tills are functioning. It's a classic example of asymmetric information, where the company is in a much better position than the customer to know the true state of affairs.

10. R.J. Ball and T. Burns, 'The inflationary mechanism in the UK economy', *American Economic Review*, 66:4 (1976).

11. It's worth noting that not all governments in the 1930s made good on their loans: every single Latin American country defaulted in that decade.

12. J. Banks and S. Tanner, *Household Saving in the UK*, Institute for Fiscal Studies, London, 1999, available at https://ifs.org.uk/publications/household-saving-uk

13. George Lazenby was the short-lived Bond number two. David Niven played Bond in the 'spoof' version of *Casino Royale*.

14. Some went earlier. The appropriately titled album *Exile on Main St.* was largely recorded by the Rolling Stones at Nellcôte, a villa in the south of France, in 1971. The Beatles complained about the 'Taxman' on their *Revolver* album in 1966.

15. The 1978–1979 Winter of Discontent suggests they were partially right.

16. Falling inflation was, itself, a reason for stronger UK growth: as it tumbled, the need to save to meet wealth targets previously eroded through inflation fell. As such, the saving ratio dropped and spending picked up.

17. 'Bank of England chief under fire for wage restraint call', *Financial Times*, 4 February 2022, available at https://www.ft.com/content/b661b0cd-2f2b-4465-882e-c62ff19bf1c8 (subscription required).

Chapter 5: How to get rid of inflation . . . and how not to

1. This is a version of the Maradona theory of interest rates, as memorably described by Mervyn King while governor of the Bank of England in his 2005 Mais Lecture, 'Monetary Policy: Practice Ahead of Theory', available at https://www.bankofengland.co.uk/-/media/boe/files/speech/2005/monetary-policy-practice-ahead-of-theory

2. See A.W. Phillips, 'The relation between unemployment and the rate of change of money wage rates in the United Kingdom, 1861–1957', *Economica*, November 1958, available at https://onlinelibrary.wiley.com/doi/epdf/10.1111/j.1468-0335.1958.tb00003.x

3. Not all countries focused on the trade-off between unemployment and inflation: in the UK, for example, the big challenge in the late 1960s in a world of fixed exchange rates and limited cross-border capital flows was managing the trade-off between unemployment and the balance of payments.

4. M. Friedman, 'The role of monetary policy', *American Economic Review*, 58:1 (1968).

5. E.S. Phelps, 'Phillips curves, expectations of inflation and optimal unemployment over time', *Economica*, 34:135 (1967).

6. See T. Sargent, 'The ends of four big inflations', in R.E. Hall (ed.), *Inflation: Causes and effects*, University of Chicago Press, Chicago, IL, 1982, available at https://www.nber.org/system/files/chapters/c11452/c11452.pdf

7. There are similarities with the world of Covid lockdowns. In normal circumstances, lockdowns would be totally unacceptable, but in the midst of a nasty pandemic, the majority are prepared to acquiesce. In other words, policy options depend on a nation's specific circumstances at a particular point in time.

8. North Sea oil was, in effect, a windfall gain for the UK economy – even more so following the doubling of the oil price in the wake of the 1979 Iranian Revolution; however, resources had to be diverted away from less 'rewarding' areas of economic endeavour. The exchange rate was one mechanism through which this was achieved. Unfortunately, this led to the partial destruction of manufacturing industry (notably in the Midlands), and with it a huge increase in unemployment. North Sea oil production was capital intensive, but used relatively few workers.

9. There are earlier examples. For example, the Babylonian Code of Hammurabi contains evidence of price controls two thousand years earlier than the Diocletian Edict.

10. A. Kropff, 'An English translation of the Edict on Maximum Prices, also known as the Price Edict of Diocletian', Academia.edu, April 2016. The threat of a punishment even more serious than the death penalty is an interesting idea.

11. Leeches were popular treatments for a range of ailments, and were sometimes collected by poor people who used their own bodies as 'human traps'. Toshers, meanwhile, spent their time in the sewers trawling through effluent in the hope of finding an accidentally discarded item of value. Some were, apparently, rather successful, even if they were, at the same time, rather smelly.

12. C. Whiteman, 'A new investigation of the impact of wage and price controls', *Federal Reserve Bank of Minneapolis Quarterly Review*, Spring 1978.

13. For a dialogue on these issues, see M. Sandbu, 'Central bankers should think twice before pressing the brake even harder', *Financial Times*, 19 April 2022; and S. King, 'Letter: Policymakers should recall the lessons of the 1970s oil crisis', *Financial Times*, 28 April 2022, available respectively at https://www.ft.com/content/41c248a2-4d30-4a47-a10c-7e37459e1829 and https://www.ft.com/content/8b237789-dcfa-4499-bfb7-f52ac9dc4ad1 (subscription required).

14. See I. Weber, 'Could strategic price controls help fight inflation?', *Guardian*, 29 December 2021, available at https://www.theguardian.com/business/commentisfree/2021/dec/29/inflation-price-controls-time-we-use-it and T.N. Tucker, 'Price controls: How the US has used them and how they can help shape industries', Roosevelt Institute,

November 2021, available at https://rooseveltinstitute.org/wp-content/uploads/2021/11/RI_Industrial-Policy-Price-Controls_Brief-202111.pdf

15. See S. King, 'Fighting inflation: Are price controls about to make a comeback?', HSBC Global Research, January 2022, available at https://www.research.hsbc.com/C/1/1/320/qjcVtbb

16. See H. Rockoff, *Drastic Measures: A history of wage and price controls in the United States*, Cambridge University Press, Cambridge, 1984.

17. Indeed, to the extent that Chinese and Indian demand for Russian energy continued to rise – thereby boosting the price and value of Russian exports – the effect of western sanctions in damaging the Russian economy was markedly reduced.

18. In effect, by driving wholesale prices higher, subsidies serve not to protect the living standards of those who are supposed to benefit, but instead to raise revenues for gas producers worldwide, including those of the malevolent variety.

19. Although see chapter 7: it's not at all clear that today's independent central banks would have had the political authority to tackle high inflation in the late 1970s and early 1980s.

20. For a detailed discussion of potential drivers of inflation in 2021 and onwards, see R. Reis, 'The burst of high inflation in 2021–2022: How and why did we get here?', CEPR Press Discussion Paper No.17514 (2002), available at https://cepr.org/publications/dp17514

21. For a marginally technical, yet highly amusing, summary of the expectations 'problem', see J.B. Rudd, 'Why do we think that inflation expectations matter for inflation? (And should we?)', Finance and Economics Discussion Series, Divisions of Research & Statistics and Monetary Affairs, Federal Reserve Board, Washington, DC, September 2021, available at https://www.federalreserve.gov/econres/feds/files/2021062pap.pdf

22. The Glazer family owns Manchester United, but has not been popular with many of the fans. This particular chant was sung during a match at Old Trafford in January 2020, which resulted in a 2-0 defeat to lowly Burnley. *Daily Star*, 23 January 2020, available at https://www.dailystar.co.uk/sport/football/every-anti-glazer-chant-belted-21342055

Chapter 6: Four inflationary tests

1. Some have claimed that there are similarities between the post-pandemic inflation and the post-Second World War experience. See, for example, F.S. Mandelman, 'Money aggregates, debt, pent-up demand and inflation: Evidence from WWII', Center for Quantitative Economic Research, Federal Reserve Bank of Atlanta, May 2021, available at https://www.atlantafed.org/-/media/documents/research/publications/policy-hub/2021/05/17/04-wwii-and-today--monetary-parallels.pdf

2. A. Barber, 'Remarks during industrial and economic situation debate', House of Commons, 6 February 1974, available at https://www.theyworkforyou.com/debates/?id=1974-02-06a.1233.1

3. Hansard, House of Commons Debates, 26 March 1974, vol. 871, cc282–9, available at https://api.parliament.uk/historic-hansard/commons/1974/mar/26/the-economic-outlook

4. ibid.

5. https://www.theyworkforyou.com/search/?pid=16553&pop=1

6. Most obviously, the UK adherence to broad money aggregates – reflecting the slippery nature of the relationship between non-interest-bearing narrow money and the interest-bearing deposits contained within broad money – led to counterintuitive results: higher interest rates increased demand for time deposits, boosting money supply, when the ambition was to do exactly the opposite. Moreover, inflation started to decline even as monetary growth remained robust.

7. Goodhart's Law, named after Charles Goodhart, its author, states that 'any observed statistical regularity will tend to collapse once pressure is placed upon it for control purposes'.

8. J.B. Taylor, 'Discretion versus policy rules in practice', *Carnegie-Rockefeller Conference Series on Public Policy*, 39 (1993), available at http://web.stanford.edu/~johntayl/Papers/Discretion.PDF

9. See, for example, S. King, 'The credibility gap', *HSBC Research*, September 2008, available (to HSBC clients) at https://www.research.hsbc.com/R/10/VQ3gpj8Qjohf

10. Some have also gone back in time, in some cases revealing that, whatever the rule, inflation in the 1970s would have been difficult to defeat. See L. Benati, 'The "Great Moderation" in the United Kingdom', *Journal of Money, Credit and Banking*, 40:1 (2008).

11. See, for example, C. Bean, 'Globalisation and inflation', Speech to the LSE Economics Society, Bank of England, October 2006, available at https://www.bankofengland.co.uk/-/media/boe/files/speech/2006/globalisation-and-inflation

12. J.H. Stock and M.W. Watson, 'Has the business cycle changed and why?', in M. Gertler and K. Rogoff (eds), *NBER Macroeconomics Annual 2002*, Vol. 17, MIT Press, Cambridge, MA, 2002.

13. For an early defence of the approach – and for a defence of the use of forecasts more generally – see A. Budd, 'Economic policy, with and without forecasts', The Sir Alec Cairncross Lecture, November 1998, available at https://www.bankofengland.co.uk/-/media/boe/files/speech/1998/economic-policy-with-and-without-forecasts.pdf

14. See, for example, L.E.O. Svensson, 'Monetary policy strategies for the Federal Reserve', *International Journal of Central Banking*, February 2022.

15. See 'Taylor Rule utility', Center for Quantitative Economic Research, Federal Reserve Bank of Atlanta, available at https://www.atlantafed.org/cqer/research/taylor-rule?panel=1

16. B. Broadbent, 'Lags, trade-offs and the challenges facing monetary policy', Speech given at the Leeds University Business School, December 2021, available at https://www.bankofengland.co.uk/-/media/boe/files/speech/2021/december/lags-trade-offs-and-the-challenges-facing-monetary-policy-speech-by-ben-broadbent.pdf

17. Oral evidence provided to the Treasury Committee of the House of Commons on Monday, 16 May 2002, available at https://committees.parliament.uk/oralevidence/10215/pdf/

18. M. King, 'Monetary policy in a world of radical uncertainty', Institute of International Monetary Research Annual Public Lecture, November 2021.

19. With notes and coin offering a guaranteed zero nominal interest rate, significantly negative interest rates on bank deposits are tricky to impose, let alone maintain: at the limit, people would withdraw their money from the banking system, prompting its collapse.

20. This is not universally true: the Bank of England's chief economist, Huw Pill, warned after the Kwarteng 'minibudget' in September 2022 that the bank might have to take more aggressive action to deal with the potential inflationary consequences of a looser fiscal stance. In the event, however, the bank was forced the very next day into buying large amounts of government debt to prevent a gilt-market meltdown.

21. S. King, 'Bubble trouble', HSBC, London, 1999.

22. S. Tenreyro, 'Monetary policy during pandemics: Inflation before, during and after Covid-19', Bank of England, April 2020, available at https://www.bankofengland.co.uk/-/media/boe/files/speech/2020/monetary-policy-during-pandemics.pdf

23. M. Saunders, 'Covid-19 and monetary policy', Bank of England, May 2020, available at https://www.bankofengland.co.uk/-/media/boe/files/speech/2020/covid-19-and-monetary-policy-speech-by-michael-saunders.pdf

24. G. Vlieghe, 'An update on the economic outlook', Bank of England, February 2021, available at https://www.bankofengland.co.uk/-/media/boe/files/speech/2021/february/an-update-on-the-economic-outlook-speech-by-gertjan-vlieghe.pdf

25. J. Powell, 'Monetary policy in the time of COVID', at the Macroeconomic Policy in an Uneven Economy economic policy symposium sponsored by the Federal Reserve Bank of Kansas City, Jackson Hole, WY, available at https://www.federalreserve.gov/newsevents/speech/powell20210827a.htm

26. There's a ghoulish connection between the attitudes of central bankers and those in the Soviet Union with responsibility for nuclear energy: in the days after the Chernobyl disaster, there was a refusal in the upper echelons of the corridors of power to believe that the accident could possibly have happened.

Chapter 7: Lessons, warnings and possible next steps

1. Part of the problem with the Truss government's fiscal plan was uncertainty regarding a Bank of England response.

2. Some central banks switched to quantitative tightening as inflation picked up – selling assets on their balance sheets and, in the process, mopping up liquidity. None, however, has explicitly abandoned quantitative easing over the long term, implying that renewed periods of economic weakness could see its return.

3. G. Lyons, 'Why Truss's plans for fiscal easing are affordable, non-inflationary – and necessary', conservativehome, September 2022, available at https://conservativehome.com/2022/09/06/gerard-lyons-why-trusss-plans-for-fiscal-easing-are-not-inflationary-but-necessary/

4. Central banks will still need to act on occasion as 'lenders of last resort', but such occasions should be seen as the exception, rather than the rule.

5. See 'ECB Knowledge & Attitudes Survey 2021', conducted by Kantar Belgium SA, at the request of the European Central Bank, January 2022, available at https://www.ecb.europa.eu/ecb/access_to_documents/document/pa_document/shared/data/ecb.dr.par2022_0007_knowledge_attitudes_survey2021.en.pdf

6. See 'Bank of England/Ipsos Inflation Attitudes Survey – August 2022', available at https://www.bankofengland.co.uk/inflation-attitudes-survey/2022/august-2022. Scroll down the page to find a link to a spreadsheet with a full history of data back to 1999.

7. See, for example, B.S. Bernanke, *21st Century Monetary Policy: The Federal Reserve from the Great Inflation to COVID-19*, Norton, New York, 2022, especially chapter 2, 'Burns and Volcker'.

8. There were significant risks with this approach, notably the failure of Continental Illinois in 1984, and later the Savings and Loan crisis. Ridding a country of inflation exposes a range of financial weaknesses that might otherwise have remained dormant.

9. I wonder if, in time, the Truss Experiment will be regarded as the British right-wing equivalent of Mitterrand's socialist version.

10. At the time, the calibration of monetary policy was complicated by the degree of structural change taking place within the financial sector.

11. Federal Reserve Press Release, 15 December 2021, available at https://www.federalreserve.gov/monetarypolicy/files/monetary20211215a1.pdf

12. See 'Bank Rate maintained at 0.1% – September 2021, Monetary Policy Summary and minutes of the Monetary Policy Committee meeting', available at https://www.bankofengland.co.uk/monetary-policy-summary-and-minutes/2021/september-2021

13. Two members of the nine-person committee – Dave Ramsden and Michael Saunders – voted to end asset purchases, thus bringing quantitative easing to an end, but no one voted in favour of higher interest rates.

14. See 'A history of FOMC Dissents', Federal Reserve Bank of St Louis, available at https://www.stlouisfed.org/fomcspeak/history-fomc-dissents
15. See 'Monetary Policy Committee Voting History', Bank of England, accessible via a link on successive 'Monetary Policy Summary' webpages. As an example, the summary dated 22 September 2022 is available at https://www.bankofengland.co.uk/monetary-policy-summary-and-minutes/2022/september-2022. The 'dissenters' in 2008 were the 'hawkish' Professor Tim Besley and the 'dovish' Professor David Blanchflower.
16. See, for example, G.B. Eggertsson, 'How to fight deflation in a liquidity trap: Committing to being irresponsible', IMF Working Paper WP/03/64, Washington, DC, 2003, available at https://www.imf.org/external/pubs/ft/wp/2003/wp0364.pdf or G.B. Eggertsson and M. Woodford, 'The zero bound on interest rates and optimal monetary policy', *Brookings Papers on Economic Activity*, 1 (2003), available at https://www.brookings.edu/wp-content/uploads/2003/01/2003a_bpea_eggertsson.pdf
17. 'Chapter 1: Old challenges, new shocks', Bank for International Settlements Annual Economic Report, June 2022, available at https://www.bis.org/publ/arpdf/ar2022e1.htm
18. At the time of writing, however, gold remains in the doldrums, suggesting that investors still believe inflation will be well behaved over the medium term.
19. Sterling's collapse in the mid-1970s is a case in point.
20. Per Jacobsson was a Swedish economist and managing director of the IMF between 1956 and his death in 1963. The two lectures are, respectively, A.F. Burns, 'The anguish of central banking' (1979) and P.A. Volcker, 'The triumph of central banking?' (1990), both available at http://www.perjacobsson.org/lectures.htm

Bibliography

Alt, J.E., *The Politics of Economic Decline: Economic management and political behaviour in Britain since 1964*, Cambridge University Press, Cambridge, 1979

Arrow, K. and G. Debreu, 'Existence of an equilibrium for a competitive economy', *Econometrica*, 22:3 (1954)

Ball, R.J. and T. Burns, 'The inflationary mechanism in the UK economy', *American Economic Review*, 66:4 (1976)

Banks, J. and S. Tanner, *Household Saving in the UK*, Institute for Fiscal Studies, London, 1999, available at https://ifs.org.uk/publications/household-saving-uk

Bean, C., 'Globalisation and inflation', Speech to the LSE Economics Society, Bank of England, October 2006, available at https://www.bankofengland.co.uk/-/media/boe/files/speech/2006/globalisation-and-inflation

Benati, L., 'The "Great Moderation" in the United Kingdom', *Journal of Money, Credit and Banking*, 40:1 (2008).

Bernanke, B., 'Remarks by Governor Ben S. Bernanke at the conference to honor Milton Friedman', University of Chicago, Illinois, 8 November 2002, available at https://www.federalreserve.gov/boarddocs/speeches/2002/20021108/

Bernanke, B., 'The Great Moderation: Remarks at the meetings of the Eastern Economic Association', February 2004, available at https://www.federalreserve.gov/boarddocs/speeches/2004/20040220/

Bernanke, B., *21st Century Monetary Policy: The Federal Reserve from the Great Inflation to COVID-19*, Norton, New York, 2022

Bernanke, B. and H. James, 'The gold standard, deflation, and financial crisis in the Great Depression: An international comparison' (1991), in B. Bernanke, *Essays on the Great Depression*, Princeton University Press, Princeton, NJ, 2004

Blanchard, O., A. Domash and L. Summers, 'Bad news for the Fed from the Beveridge space', Policy Brief, Peterson Institute for International Economics, Washington, DC, July 2002, available at https://www.piie.com/sites/default/files/documents/pb22-7.pdf

Bootle, R., *The Death of Inflation: Surviving and thriving in the zero era*, Nicholas Brealey Publishing, London, 1996

Brainard, W., 'Uncertainty and the effectiveness of policy', *American Economic Review*, 57:2 (1967), Papers and Proceedings of the Seventy-ninth Annual Meeting of the American Economic Association

Broadbent, B., 'Lags, trade-offs and the challenges facing monetary policy', Speech given at the Leeds University Business School, December 2021, available at https://www.bankofengland.co.uk/-/media/boe/files/speech/2021/december/lags-trade-offs-and-the-challenges-facing-monetary-policy-speech-by-ben-broadbent.pdf

Budd, A., 'Economic policy, with and without forecasts', The Sir Alec Cairncross Lecture, November 1998, available at https://www.bankofengland.co.uk/-/media/boe/files/speech/1998/economic-policy-with-and-without-forecasts.pdf

Burns, A.F., 'The anguish of central banking' (1979), available at http://www.perjacobsson.org/lectures/1979.pdf

Calomiris, C. and J. Mason, 'Consequences of bank distress during the Great Depression', *American Economic Review*, 93:3 (2003)

Campbell, C.D. and G. Tullock, 'Hyperinflation in China, 1937–49', *Journal of Political Economy*, 62:3 (1954)

Capie, F.H. (ed.), *Major Inflations in History*, Edward Elgar, Aldershot, 1991

Congdon, T., 'Letter: Let's revive the seventies habit of targeting the money supply', *Financial Times*, 8 March 2021, available at https://www.ft.com/content/ff9b7393-f6ed-4b05-8873-1fe197181ba0 (subscription required)

Cookson, R., 'Brace yourself for a sharp rise in inflation', Bloomberg, November 2020, available at https://finance.yahoo.com/news/inflation-may-pick-sharply-060002710.html

De Waal, E., *The Hare with Amber Eyes: A hidden inheritance*, Vintage, London, 2011

The Economist, 'Argentina's new, honest inflation statistics: The end of bogus accounting', 25 May 2017, available at https://www.economist.com/the-americas/2017/05/25/argentinas-new-honest-inflation-statistics

Eggertsson, G.B., 'How to fight deflation in a liquidity trap: Committing to being irresponsible', IMF Working Paper WP/03/64, Washington, DC, 2003, available at https://www.imf.org/external/pubs/ft/wp/2003/wp0364.pdf

Eggertsson, G.B. and M. Woodford, 'The zero bound on interest rates and optimal monetary policy', *Brookings Papers on Economic Activity*, 1 (2003), available at https://www.brookings.edu/wp-content/uploads/2003/01/2003a_bpea_eggertsson.pdf

Eggleston, G.C., *A Rebel's Recollections* (1875), reprinted by Indiana University Press, Bloomington, IN, 1959

Eichengreen, B., *Golden Fetters: The gold standard and the Great Depression 1919–1939* (NBER Series on Long-term Factors in Economic Development), Oxford University Press, New York/Oxford, 1992

Figura, A. and C. Waller, 'What does the Beveridge curve tell us about the likelihood of a soft landing?', FEDS Notes, Board of Governors of the Federal Reserve System, 29 July 2022, available at https://www.federalreserve.gov/econres/notes/feds-notes/what-does-the-beveridge-curve-tell-us-about-the-likelihood-of-a-soft-landing-20220729.html

Fisher, I., assisted by H.G. Brown, *The Purchasing Power of Money: Its determination and relation to credit, interest and crisis*, Macmillan, New York, 1911

Friedman, M., 'The role of monetary policy', *American Economic Review*, 58:1 (1968)

Friedman, M. and A. Schwartz, *A Monetary History of the United States, 1867–1960*, National Bureau of Economic Research, Cambridge, MA, 1963

Goldstone, J., 'Monetary versus velocity interpretations of the "price revolution": A comment', *Journal of Economic History*, 51:1 (1991), pp. 176–181

Goodhart, C. and M. Pradhan, *The Great Demographic Reversal: Ageing societies, waning inequality and an inflation revival*, Palgrave Macmillan/Springer Nature, Cham (Switzerland), 2020

Her Majesty's Stationery Office (HMSO), 'Attack on Inflation: A Policy for Survival: A guide to the Government's Programme', Crown Copyright, August 1975, available at https://wdc.contentdm.oclc.org/digital/collection/tav/id/53

Humphrey, T.M, 'The quantity theory of money: Its historical evolution and role in policy debates', *Federal Reserve of Richmond Economic Review*, May/June 1974, available at https://core.ac.uk/download/pdf/6917453.pdf

Kelton, S., *The Deficit Myth: Modern Monetary Theory and how to build a better economy*, John Murray, London, 2020

Kelton, S., 'There are so many things we could be doing – together – to crush inflation', June 2022, available at https://stephaniekelton.substack.com/p/catch-me-on-the-mehdi-hasan-show

Keynes, J.M., 'Inflation' (1919), in E. Johnson and D. Moggridge (eds), *The Collected Writings of John Maynard Keynes*, Vol. IX, *Essays in Persuasion*, Cambridge University Press for the Royal Economic Society, 1978

Keynes, J.M., 'The economic consequences of Mr Churchill' (1925), in E. Johnson and D. Moggridge (eds), *The Collected Writings of John Maynard Keynes*, Vol. IX, *Essays in Persuasion*, Cambridge University Press for the Royal Economic Society, 1978

Keynes, J.M., *How to Pay for the War: A radical plan for the chancellor of the Exchequer*, Macmillan and Co. Limited, London, 1940, available at https://fraser.stlouisfed.org/files/docs/historical/Misc/howtopayforthewar_1940.pdf

King, M., 'Monetary Policy: Practice Ahead of Theory', Mais Lecture, 2005, available at https://www.bankofengland.co.uk/-/media/boe/files/speech/2005/monetary-policy-practice-ahead-of-theory

King, M., *The End of Alchemy: Money, banking and the future of the global economy*, Little, Brown, London, 2016

King, M., 'Monetary policy in a world of radical uncertainty', Institute of International Monetary Research Annual Public Lecture, November 2021

King, S.D., 'Bubble trouble', HSBC, London, 1999

King, S.D., 'The credibility gap', *HSBC Research*, September 2008, available (to HSBC clients) at https://www.research.hsbc.com/R/10/VQ3gpj8Qjohf

King, S.D., *Grave New World: The end of globalization, the return of history*, revised edition, Yale University Press, London, 2018

King, S.D., 'Despite what central bankers say we're right to worry about inflation', *Evening Standard*, May 2021, available at https://www.standard.co.uk/comment/comment/despite-central-bankers-right-to-worry-inflation-b935602.html

King, S.D., 'Fighting inflation: Are price controls about to make a comeback?', HSBC Global Research, January 2022, available at https://www.research.hsbc.com/C/1/1/320/qjcVtbb

King, S.D., 'Letter: Policymakers should recall the lessons of the 1970s oil crisis', *Financial Times*, 28 April 2022, available at https://www.ft.com/content/8b237789-dcfa-4499-bfb7-f52ac9dc4ad1 (subscription required)

Kropff, A., 'An English translation of the Edict on Maximum Prices, also known as the Price Edict of Diocletian', Academia.edu, April 2016

Levenson, T., *Money for Nothing: The South Sea Bubble and the invention of modern capitalism*, Random House, New York, 2020

Lyons, G., 'Why Truss's plans for fiscal easing are affordable, non-inflationary – and necessary', conservativehome, September 2022, available at https://conservativehome.com/2022/09/06/gerard-lyons-why-trusss-plans-for-fiscal-easing-are-not-inflationary-but-necessary/

Mandelman, F.S., 'Money aggregates, debt, pent-up demand and inflation: Evidence from WWII', Center for Quantitative Economic Research, Federal Reserve Bank of Atlanta, May 2021, available at https://www.atlantafed.org/-/media/documents/research/publications/policy-hub/2021/05/17/04-wwii-and-today--monetary-parallels.pdf

Office for Budget Responsibility, 'Debt maturity, quantitative easing and interest rate sensitivity', Economic and Fiscal Outlook, March 2021, available at https://obr.uk/box/debt-maturity-quantitative-easing-and-interest-rate-sensitivity/

Paarlberg, D., *An Analysis and History of Inflation*, Praeger, Westport, CT, 1993

Pamuk, S., 'Prices in the Ottoman Empire, 1469–1914', *International Journal of Middle East Studies*, 36 (2004)

Panetta, F., 'Normalising monetary policy in non-normal times', policy lecture hosted by the SAFE Policy Center at Goethe University and the

Centre for Economic Policy Research, available at https://www.ecb.
europa.eu/press/key/date/2022/html/ecb.sp220525~eef274e856.en.
html

Phelps, E.S., 'Phillips curves, expectations of inflation and optimal unemployment over time', *Economica*, 34:135 (1967)

Phillips, A.W., 'The relation between unemployment and the rate of change
of money wage rates in the United Kingdom, 1861–1957', *Economica*,
November 1958, available at https://onlinelibrary.wiley.com/doi/
epdf/10.1111/j.1468-0335.1958.tb00003.x

Powell, J., 'Monetary policy in the time of COVID', at the Macroeconomic
Policy in an Uneven Economy economic policy symposium sponsored by
the Federal Reserve Bank of Kansas City, Jackson Hole, WY, available at
https://www.federalreserve.gov/newsevents/speech/powell20210827a.
htm

Robins, N. and N. Hagan, 'Mercury production and use in colonial Andean
silver production: Emissions and health implications', *Environmental
Health Perspectives*, 120:5 (2012)

Reis, R., 'The burst of high inflation in 2021–2022: How and why did we
get here?', CEPR Press Discussion Paper No.17514 (2002), available at
https://cepr.org/publications/dp17514

Rockoff, H., *Drastic Measures: A history of wage and price controls in the
United States*, Cambridge University Press, Cambridge, 1984

Rudd, J.B., 'Why do we think that inflation expectations matter for inflation? (And should we?)', Finance and Economics Discussion Series,
Divisions of Research & Statistics and Monetary Affairs, Federal Reserve
Board, Washington, DC, September 2021, available at https://www.
federalreserve.gov/econres/feds/files/2021062pap.pdf

Rugaber, C., 'Inflation ahead? Even a top economist says it's complicated',
AP News, June 2021, available at https://apnews.com/article/lifestyle-
inflation-business-536d99a7a2d7abf8dd735963e57b237f

Sandbu, M., 'Central bankers should think twice before pressing the brake
even harder', *Financial Times*, 19 April 2022, available at https://www.
ft.com/content/41c248a2-4d30-4a47-a10c-7e37459e1829 (subscription
required)

Sargent, T., 'The ends of four big inflations', in R.E. Hall (ed.), *Inflation:
Causes and effects*, University of Chicago Press, Chicago, IL, 1982,
available at https://www.nber.org/system/files/chapters/c11452/c11452.
pdf

Saunders, M., 'Covid-19 and monetary policy', Bank of England, May
2020, available at https://www.bankofengland.co.uk/-/media/boe/files/
speech/2020/covid-19-and-monetary-policy-speech-by-michael-
saunders.pdf

Schnabel, I., 'The globalisation of inflation', address to a conference organised by the Österreichische Vereinigung für Finanzanalyse und Asset
Management, available at https://www.ecb.europa.eu/press/key/date/
2022/html/ecb.sp220511_1~e9ba02e127.en.html

Smith, A., *The Wealth of Nations*, ed. A. Skinner, Penguin, London, 1982

Spang, R.L., *Stuff and Money in the Time of the French Revolution*, Harvard University Press, Cambridge, MA, 2015

Stock, J.H. and M.W. Watson, 'Has the business cycle changed and why?', in M. Gertler and K. Rogoff (eds), *NBER Macroeconomics Annual 2002*, Vol. 17, MIT Press, Cambridge, MA, 2002

Summers, L., 'The inflation risk is real', May 2021, available at http://larrysummers.com/2021/05/24/the-inflation-risk-is-real/

Svensson, L.E.O., 'Monetary policy strategies for the Federal Reserve', *International Journal of Central Banking*, February 2022

Taylor, J.B., 'Discretion versus policy rules in practice', *Carnegie-Rockefeller Conference Series on Public Policy*, 39 (1993), available at http://web.stanford.edu/~johntayl/Papers/Discretion.PDF

Tenreyro, S., 'Monetary policy during pandemics: Inflation before, during and after Covid-19', Bank of England, April 2020, available at https://www.bankofengland.co.uk/-/media/boe/files/speech/2020/monetary-policy-during-pandemics.pdf

Time, 'The Ruhr', 17 March 1923, available at https://content.time.com/time/subscriber/article/0,33009,715096,00.html

Tomlinson, J., 'British government and popular understanding of inflation in the mid-1970s', *Economic History Review*, 67:3 (2014)

Tucker, T.N., 'Price controls: How the US has used them and how they can help shape industries', Roosevelt Institute, November 2021, available at https://rooseveltinstitute.org/wp-content/uploads/2021/11/RI_Industrial-Policy-Price-Controls_Brief-202111.pdf

United States House of Representatives, 'The Legislation Placing "In God We Trust" on National Currency', Historical Highlights, History, Art & Archives, available at https://history.house.gov/Historical-Highlights/1951-2000/The-legislation-placing-%E2%80%9CIn-God-We-Trust%E2%80%9D-on-national-currency/

Vlieghe, G., 'An update on the economic outlook', Bank of England, February 2021, available at https://www.bankofengland.co.uk/-/media/boe/files/speech/2021/february/an-update-on-the-economic-outlook-speech-by-gertjan-vlieghe.pdf

Volckart, O., 'Early beginnings of the quantity theory of money and their context in Polish and Prussian monetary policies, c.1520–1550', *Economic History Review*, New Series, 50:3 (1997)

Volcker, P.A., 'The triumph of central banking?' (1990), available at http://www.perjacobsson.org/lectures/1990.pdf

Voltaire, F., *Candide, or Optimism*, trans. T. Cuffe, Penguin, London, 2006

Weber, I., 'Could strategic price controls help fight inflation?', *Guardian*, 29 December 2021, available at https://www.theguardian.com/business/commentisfree/2021/dec/29/inflation-price-controls-time-we-use-it

Whiteman, C., 'A new investigation of the impact of wage and price controls', *Federal Reserve Bank of Minneapolis Quarterly Review*, Spring 1978

Wolf, M., 'The return of the inflation spectre', *Financial Times*, 26 March 2021, available at https://www.ft.com/content/6cfb36ca-d3ce-4dd3-b70d-eecc332ba1df (subscription required)

Wolf, M., 'As inflation rises, the monetarist dog is having its day', *Financial Times*, 22 February 2022, available at https://www.ft.com/content/0cd1d666-8842-4c82-8344-07c4e433a408 (subscription required)

Wolf, M., 'Inflation is a political challenge as well as an economic one', *Financial Times*, 12 July 2022, available at https://www.ft.com/content/2022df1d-57c5-44a4-93e6-73f5f5274ca8 (subscription required)

Woodford, M., 'Public debt and the price level', Paper prepared for the Bank of England Conference on Government Debt and Monetary Policy, 18–19 June 1998, available at https://blogs.cuit.columbia.edu/mw2230/files/2017/08/BOE.pdf

INDEX